# Why the Apple Falls

# Why the Apple Falls

## Fantastic Physics for Children

Swagata Deb
and
Sandipan Deb

JUGGERNAUT BOOKS
C-I-128, First Floor, Sangam Vihar, Near Holi Chowk,
New Delhi 110080, India

First published by Juggernaut Books 2024



10 9 8 7 6 5 4 3 2 1

P-ISBN: 9789353456429
E-ISBN: 9789353456450



Illustrations on pages 7, 15, 69, 83, 90, 169 and 208
by Sayan Mukherjee

Typeset in Adobe Caslon Pro by R. Ajith Kumar, Noida

Printed at Thomson Press India Ltd

*To our late fathers Ajit Kumar Banerjee and Hrishikesh Deb, two men very different from each other but absolutely alike in their honesty, courage and affection*

# Contents


1. What Is Physics? 1
2. Ancient Physics 12
3. Eureka! Archimedes and the Golden Crown 23
4. Aryabhata the Genius 33
5. From Zero to Infinity 44
6. How Copernicus Shifted the Centre of the Universe 57
7. Galileo Galilei: The Father of Modern Science 68
8. How Newton Uncovered the Laws of Nature 75
9. The Men Who Gave Us Electricity 86
10. The Birth of Electromagnetism 95
11. The Story of Light 104
12. The Building Blocks of Matter 115
13. Heat as Energy 127
14. Invisible Rays 145

15. Things That Glow in the Dark 157
16. The Music of Waves 168
17. Einstein and a Whole New World 177
18. Does God Play Dice? 190
19. It Doesn't Matter 199
20. Smaller and Smaller Particles 213
21. The Power of the Atom 224
22. What Light Can Do for Us 239
23. Indian Physicists Who Won the Nobel Prize 248
24. . . . And the Indians Who Didn't Win 265
25. The Now and the Next 295

*A Note on the Authors* 317

# 1

# What Is Physics?

In our universe, the smallest particle scientists have discovered is a quark, a little ball that lives inside the atom and whose radius is 43 billion-billionths of a centimetre (0.43 x $10^{-16}$ cm)! The largest thing found till now is a supercluster of galaxies, called the Hercules-Corona Borealis Great Wall. It is so wide that light, which travels at the speed of 300,000 kilometres per second, takes about 10 billion years to move across the entire structure. And the universe itself is only 13.8 billion years old!

Physics is the study of everything from quarks to supergalaxies. And almost none of the things that we see and use today, from ice cream and airplanes to ceiling fans and cell phones, would have been possible without the work done by physicists.

The word 'physics' entered English in the fifteenth century, derived from the Latin word *physica*, which means 'study of nature' and the Greek *phusikē*, or 'knowledge of nature'. But till the beginning of the twentieth century, it was clubbed together with chemistry, biology, botany, geology and so on, under the broad term 'natural sciences'.

## Physics and Math

Physicists are thinkers and seekers of knowledge. They try to understand the workings of nature using mathematics, which is full of abstract ideas and equations. Physicists use higher mathematics as a tool to figure out how nature works. Indeed, a lot of higher mathematics was initially worked out to understand things that happen in the physical universe.

Take motion as an example. Motion is present everywhere in nature. From the movement of stars across the sky to the crashing of waves on the seashore and tree leaves fluttering in the wind – there is constant motion and constant change. Galileo Galilei and Sir Isaac Newton were the first scientists who tried to quantify motion and eventually discovered the laws governing moving bodies. Based on their discoveries, they were also able to explain the movement of planets, how tides happen, why an apple falls instead of going up and a whole lot of other things.

Galileo and Newton found that they could describe motion using mathematical equations. And centuries later, people used these equations to design washing machines and send rockets into space!

## Who Invented Physics?

The answer to the question 'Who invented Physics?' would be 'No one in particular', or 'A great many people in general'. Human beings have always wondered why things happen and what would happen if they did something differently. The person who discovered that fire could be produced by rubbing stones together was a physicist. So was the person who invented the wheel.

Ancient philosophers who pondered on the workings of the universe were also physicists. They did not have the instruments that we have today, which can make very accurate measurements even at an atomic level. But through deep thought, they arrived at certain truths about the universe.

There is a lot of proof that ancient Indians made discoveries that were ahead of their times when it came to the sciences. Excavations at Harappa and Mohenjo Daro, major Indus Valley Civilization cities, have unearthed tools resembling rulers crafted from ivory and shell, used to take measurements. Taking measurements is an essential part of physics.

Some of our ancient rishis came to certain conclusions that Western scientists reached much later. For example, the Indian natural scientist and philosopher **Kanada**, who lived sometime between sixth century and second century BCE, introduced the concept of atoms. He suggested that everything can be divided into smaller and smaller particles, but this subdivision cannot go on endlessly. Ultimately, one would reach particles that cannot be divided any further. Kanada went on to say that these smallest entities (which he named '*parmanu*' – the ultimate smallest particle) are eternal and that they combine in various ways to produce complex substances. This is very similar to the atomic theory of matter that British chemist John Dalton developed, which was accepted only in the early nineteenth century.

In Hindi, the term for 'nuclear bomb' is 'parmanu bomb'.

Ancient Greek philosophers pondered on the nature of the universe. They came to believe that the universe was harmonious and perfect and was governed by elegant equations. However, in those times, physics was clubbed together with theology – the study of God, religion and supernatural forces – and philosophy – the study of general questions about existence. Modern physics, which we are familiar with today, rose out of theoretical mathematics, accurate astronomy – the study of stars and planets and what goes on in space – and experiments to prove or disprove ideas. Indeed, a theory becomes a 'law' only after it has been tested and verified through experiments.

## The Scientific Method

All physicists follow the 'scientific method', which involves four steps. They 'observe' something. Then they 'hypothesize', which is to develop an idea about why that something could be happening. They 'experiment' to check if the idea is correct. Finally, based on the results of the experiments, they 'conclude' whether the idea was right, half-right or completely wrong.

The Greek philosopher Thales of Miletus, who lived in the seventh century BCE, was the first physicist in the modern sense of the word, because his explanations of nature did not involve supernatural forces. He believed that although there were many kinds of materials, the basic element present everywhere was water. The interactions of the various phases of water – solid, liquid and gas, i.e., ice, water and vapour – gave materials different properties.

He was followed by Leucippus in the fourth century BCE. He, too, opposed the idea that the gods were interfering in the universe and proposed that natural phenomena had natural causes.

Archimedes, the Greek mathematician, scientist and engineer who lived in the third century BCE, is one of the most outstanding characters in the story of physics. He is best known for his 'Eureka' moment while having a bath, when he discovered the principles of density and flotation – why some solids (like a stone) sink in water and others (like leaves) float. Although this is his most popular story, Archimedes didn't stop there. He made many other important contributions to physics. He improved upon the mechanism of pulleys and levers, and laid down mathematical principles that enabled the construction of complex machines.

Mathematicians of ancient India often used their knowledge to make accurate astronomical predictions. Aryabhata was a renowned mathematician and astronomer who lived during the fifth–sixth century CE. He correctly proposed that the earth is round, rotates around its own axis and revolves around the sun. European physicists came to the same conclusions hundreds of years later and were persecuted and almost killed for saying so. Aryabhata explained how solar and lunar eclipses occur and gave an accurate measurement of the length of a day which is amazingly close to the modern estimates. Other Indian greats included Bhaskara, Brahmagupta, Varahamihira and Madhava.

Source: From 'LIDAR and Ground Ozone Measurements in the PBL during the August 11, 1999, Solar Eclipse' via researchgate.net

*The moon comes between the sun and the earth, and casts a shadow over the earth. Where the moon does not fully block off the sun, there is a partial solar eclipse. Where the sun is fully obscured by the moon, there is a total solar eclipse.*

We will look at some of these great minds later in the book.

## The Earth Moves around the Sun

Copernicus was a Polish astronomer who lived in the fifteenth century. He was the first European to propose the 'Heliocentric Theory', which states that the sun is at the centre of the solar system and that the earth and all the other planets revolve around it. This was a revolutionary idea at that time, because people believed that the earth was at the centre of the universe, and it was the sun that revolved around it. Copernicus' 'Heliocentric Theory' laid the foundation upon which Galileo and Newton could develop physics further.

Nearly a thousand years before Copernicus, Aryabhata had proposed the same theory, but by the time of Copernicus, Aryabhata's work had been forgotten outside India. In Chapter 4, we'll see why that happened. Even in India, hardly anyone remembered him.

So these are the early physicists, some of the heroes in our story. This is a story filled with many twists and turns, featuring brilliant men and women whose ideas have changed the way we look at the world. It is also closely linked to the story of technology and innovation. While physics tries to explain the workings of the universe, technology uses this knowledge for practical purposes. At the same time, physics experiments today use a lot of technology, so progress in one field has led to progress in the other.

This book is about the evolution of one of the most fascinating fields of study, from the earliest days several thousands of years ago to the latest puzzles that scientists are now trying to solve. It is also the story of some of the greatest scientists ever born – both those who have become legends and those who never got their due recognition in their lifetimes for the great discoveries they made.

**A warning: As we progress through the book, the universe will become more and more mysterious and weird!**

### The Laws of Physics

Physics is the science of matter, motion and energy. Its laws are expressed as mathematical equations. The most famous equation of all time, of course, is Albert Einstein's $E=MC^2$.

Physics can be divided into two parts: classical and quantum. Classical physics is about the movement of macroscopic objects – roughly, stuff that we can see around us – and other phenomena like heat, sound, electricity, magnetism and light. Quantum physics looks at the basic building blocks of matter, such as electrons, protons and neutrons – particles that live inside an atom.

The ultimate aim of physics is to find one set of laws that governs matter, motion and energy – from sub-atomic levels too tiny to even imagine to the extragalactic scale so vast that the mind boggles. This will be the one Grand Unified Theory that would explain everything in the universe. But it has not yet been found. Perhaps it never will be.

Even if a unified 'Law of Physics' is discovered, in science, all laws are open to being tested and re-tested based on new data and observations. This means such laws are open to be improved upon or disproved in the future. This is a basic principle of science. So the journey for knowledge never ends. And that is a beautiful thing.

# 2

# Ancient Physics

As soon as primitive humans learned to ask questions, they would have tried to understand why things happened the way they did. Why did the sun always rise in the morning in a particular direction? Why did water come pouring down from the sky sometimes? It was because of our curious minds and our thirst for knowledge that all the sciences, including physics, came into being.

In the ancient days, knowledge was passed down orally from generation to generation. So it could get lost easily, and facts could get distorted. Two factors greatly contributed to the development of the sciences – the pursuit of agriculture and the development of writing. The turning point came about 12,000 years ago, when humans discovered agriculture and how to grow food. Now, they no longer had to go out and look for food every day and were freed from focusing solely on survival. So they had the time to think about things. And with the invention of writing, it became easier to store and share thoughts, ideas and knowledge accurately. These two developments allowed people to pursue knowledge for its own sake.

Several ancient civilizations have left their mark on the development of physics, including Indian, Mesopotamian, Egyptian, Persian, Greek, Roman and Chinese. While Mesopotamia and Egypt did not contribute directly to the development of physics, their contributions to the early development of mathematics and astronomy were foundational in paving the way for later physicists, who would use this knowledge to discover the deeper laws of physics.

## Zero and One

Ancient India had not only seers and sages who wrote great philosophical works, such as the Vedas and Upanishads, but also brilliant scholars and scientists who significantly shaped our understanding of mathematics and physics. As many of us know, the concept of zero

– fundamental to our current number system – was first introduced by the great Indian mathematician Brahmagupta, in the seventh century CE.

The **zero** is possibly the most fundamental discovery in mathematics. We use it to easily convey much of the universe, from atoms to supergalaxies. The absence of zero would profoundly limit our world; many of the everyday innovations that we take for granted would simply not be possible. Without the zero, the foundation of modern technology – computers, televisions and the digital world we rely on – would crumble. Plus, advanced fields like calculus, the backbone of modern engineering, would not exist.

The decimal system was also invented in ancient India. We're all familiar with it because it helps us write big numbers with great ease. Physicists also find the decimal system useful because it allows them to express their readings accurately.

The ancient Romans did not know either the zero or the decimal system. For instance, 107 in Roman numerals is CVII. The number 99 is XCIX. Think how difficult it must have been to add CVII to XCIX, even for college graduates!

Then there's the **binary system**, on which computers and all electronics rely. Binary numbers were first described by the Vedic scholar Pingala. The system is

based on just two digits – zero and one. So, 1, 2, 3 and 4 are 01, 10, 11 and 100, and 50 is 110010. Why is it useful to use just those two numbers, you may ask? Well, an electrical current is either on or off, and we can easily use one and zero to describe those two states. When you watch a film on Netflix, it is the binary system at work, creating all the colours and sounds on your screen. Even the WhatsApp message that travels thousands of miles from a satellite high up in the sky to your phone is ultimately a stream of binary code.

## Everything Is Numbers

Among the Europeans, the Greeks were the first to attempt to give a rational explanation for the mysteries of nature. Early Greeks had begun to speculate about the fundamental substances that make up our world.

As we mentioned earlier, Thales of Miletus, who lived in the seventh century BCE, was the first Greek who tried to explain natural phenomena without referring to supernatural forces. He believed that the interactions of the various phases of water gave materials different properties. Of course, we know today that this is not true at all. But even this wrong theory shows that the ancients were pondering deeply on the nature of substances.

Pythagoras, who lived around 500 BCE, and his followers formed a religious group devoted to the study of numbers. They believed that *everything* could be reduced to numbers and that the basis of the entire universe was mathematics. Pythagoras was fascinated by the relationship between the lengths of the strings of musical instruments and the tones they produced. He found that harmonic tones were produced by two different strings if their lengths bore a simple ratio to each other. He suggested that the distances of different planets from the earth also bore a simple ratio to each other and that the planets moved in harmony.

However, we now know that this was far from the truth.

## Light of the World

Persia was another great seat of science and learning. Ancient Persian scientists and scholars proposed some groundbreaking concepts including the heliocentric model of the solar system (that the planets revolve around the sun or Helios), the finite speed of light and the idea of gravity.

The work of Abu Ali al-Hassan ibn-Haytham, an Arab mathematician, astronomer and physicist, in the eleventh century revolutionized our understanding of vision. Sometimes referred to as the father of optics – the study of light – he conducted experiments with lenses and mirrors and demonstrated that we are able to see things because light falls on these things and is reflected into our eyes. This challenged the long-held belief that our eyes emit light and illuminate objects.

Another Persian scholar, Al-Biruni, proposed that the speed of light is finite – that it can be measured and observed that light travels faster than sound. That is why sometimes on stormy nights, we see the flash of distant lightning in the sky first and hear the sound of the thunder associated with that flash quite a bit later.

Kamal al-Din Al Farizi, a Persian mathematician,

is regarded as the first person to give a satisfactory explanation of how rainbows are formed. When sunlight, which is made up of seven colours invisible to the naked eye, passes through a raindrop, it bends (called 'refraction') and then reflects off from inside the drop. As the different colours bend at different angles, the sunlight separates into a vibrant spectrum of the seven colours, which we see as a beautiful arc.

## Yin and Yang

Ancient China, too, arrived at certain conclusions that modern physics has accepted only in the past century.

Niels Bohr, the twentieth-century Danish physicist who played a key role in developing quantum theory and understanding the structure of the atom, recognized this fascinating correlation between ancient Chinese thought and modern findings in physics. The Chinese concepts of 'yin' and 'yang', which literally mean the 'dark side' and the 'sunny side' of a hill, represent the opposites that make up the world – for example, light and dark, male and female, heaven and earth and so on. Experiments in modern physics show that subatomic particles sometimes behave like waves and sometimes like particles. These two behaviours seem to

Source: Wikimedia Commons

complement each other in the same way that yin and yang complement each other.

The ancient Chinese also invented many useful things like paper and silk. Their most important invention related to physics is the magnetic compass. This was first used in city planning and later in map making and navigating ships. The compass fundamentally changed how humans understood and explored their world.

## Theories Can Be Wrong

Over time, many theories of physics have been proven wrong or incomplete, requiring modifications. That is the basic nature of human knowledge. As civilization progresses, we get to know more and more clearly how the universe works.

Some of the things that physicists believe to be true today may be proved wrong in the future. And the physicists know this.

Aristotle, who lived in the fourth century BCE, was one of the greatest Greek philosophers. He was also the childhood tutor of Alexander the Great of Macedonia. He made important contributions in the fields of logic, psychology, political science and biology. Today, more than 2,000 years after his death, his ideas continue to influence human thought. But Aristotle was not very good at – or perhaps not interested in – mathematics, so his theories about the motion of bodies up in the sky and objects on earth were hopelessly off the mark.

For many centuries, the general belief was that the earth was the centre of the universe and everything else – the sun, stars, other planets – revolved around it. Today, we know that this is absolutely incorrect.

Then there was the concept of ether, an invisible substance that we can't sense the way we feel air, see light or hear sound. It was proposed that ether permeated all of the universe and everything moved through it. However, experiments conducted over the years have shown that no such thing exists.

At one point, it was believed that the atom was the smallest particle of matter. Nothing could be smaller than the atom. Today scientists have discovered more than **200 sub-atomic particles**. In fact, there is a long list of theories about how things work at the atomic level that have been proven false.

Even Albert Einstein, the greatest physicist of the twentieth century, believed that the universe on the whole had a given size – that it wasn't growing or expanding. But astronomers discovered that the universe is, in fact, ever-expanding, growing in size all the time. When he looked at the evidence, Einstein accepted the expanding universe theory.

By definition, a theory can be considered 'scientific' only when it is 'falsifiable'. This means that at some point in the future, *it can be proved wrong* if contrary evidence is discovered. If someone says, 'I believe this is the truth and I don't want any arguments about it,' that is not a scientific theory.

And that is the beauty of physics. It is a never-ending journey with new sights popping up every once in a while. The map keeps changing, so you say, 'Oops, I took the wrong turn there! Let me just go back and try again!' or 'Hey, there's a better path that's just opened up, so let's take that!'

# 3

# Eureka! Archimedes and the Golden Crown

Syracuse is a city on the island of Sicily, today part of Italy. Hiero II, a king of Syracuse who lived in the third century BCE, had bought a golden crown, which he wanted to place on the head of the statue of a god or goddess. Suspecting that the goldsmith had cheated him, he asked the Greek polymath Archimedes – a polymath is a person of wide and varied learning – to find out whether the crown was made of pure gold or had some cheaper metals mixed into it. But since this was a holy object, Archimedes could not take it apart or disturb it in any way.

Archimedes was trying to figure out a way to solve this puzzle when one day, while in his bathtub, a brilliant solution came to him. He saw that as he lowered his body into the bathtub, the level of the water in the tub kept rising. He figured out that the volume of the water that rose would be equal to the volume of his body under water. This discovery would allow him to crack the golden crown problem.

He decided that he would put some gold, with weight exactly equal to that of the crown, into a bowl of water. He would note down exactly how much the level of water rose. He would then take the gold out of the bowl and put the king's crown in its place. If the crown was pure gold, the water would rise to the same level. But if it was impure, it would be bulkier, and the water would rise a bit more. Archimedes was so excited by his discovery that he jumped out of his tub and ran naked through the streets shouting, 'Eureka! Eureka!' – 'I found it! I found it!'

The actual events were possibly not so dramatic. But Archimedes did exist and was one of the greatest physicists and mathematicians ever. Quite a lot of our modern world runs on his original discoveries.

## Water and War

Archimedes lived during what is called the Hellenistic period. This is the 300 years of Mediterranean history between the death of Alexander the Great in 323 BCE and the emergence of the Roman Empire in 31 BCE. The word 'Hellenistic' comes from 'Hellas', the original name of Greece (modern Greece is still officially named the Hellenic Republic).

The centre of Hellenistic science was the city of Alexandria in Egypt, which was founded by Alexander the Great in 331 BCE and named after him. Indeed, Egyptian kings during that period were also of Greek origin. The wealth of Egypt and the generous support of its kings attracted well-known scholars from Athens. It is believed that Archimedes paid at least one visit to Alexandria.

There was a difference in the way the scholars of Athens and those of Alexandria approached science. Scholars in Athens tried to build theories to explain everything, but they were not too interested in experimental proofs. The scholars of Alexandria, on the other hand, focused on specific phenomena and tried to find concrete natural explanations for them. While scientists before the Hellenistic era pursued knowledge for its own sake, now they were able to apply this knowledge to the advancement of technology.

Archimedes was the most prominent scientist-technologist of this era and certainly one of the founding fathers of modern physics. He is the inventor of mechanics – the study of motion – and hydrostatics – the study of fluids at rest. These are two basic fields of physics. The **centre of gravity**, which is the point in a body through which gravity acts, was a concept that he thought up.

This is a very important concept in physics because it greatly simplifies calculations related to gravity and dynamics, the study of moving objects. It is the location of the centre of gravity of a structure – say, a building or a bridge, or even a heavily loaded ship – which tells us if the structure is stable or not. If the centre of gravity is too high, a building may topple or a ship may capsize.

Archimedes invented a variety of screws and pulleys for practical purposes. One of his inventions was a large screw that was used to lift water from rivers. It stayed in use for centuries before people came up with better methods. Archimedes also studied levers and laid down the principles by which we calculate the power of a lever. Levers had been in use for many years before Archimedes, but he used mathematics to work out the minimum effort needed to raise massive weights and how to devise such a lever system. Today, we use lever systems everywhere. For instance, when our car has a flat tyre, we use a small jack to raise the car and change the tyre. Without the jack, we would never be able to lift the car on our own. Of course, Archimedes didn't invent the car jack, but he discovered the basic rules that made it possible.

He also invented many instruments of war. The '**claw**' was a sort of giant crane with a grappling hook at its end. It could grab a part of an enemy ship, lift it up in the air and upturn it. When the Romans attacked Syracuse by sea, the claw was used to destroy many of their ships. Then there were the huge catapults that could throw boulders at ships and sink them. It is also speculated that it was Archimedes who built curved mirrors that could reflect focused sunlight on wooden ships and set them on fire.

His greatest achievement, however, remains his work on floating bodies. The insight that solved the golden crown problem is now known as the Archimedes Principle. It is one of the most fundamental laws of physics and is used for all sorts of purposes – from designing ships and submarines to checking the purity of the milk that we buy.

Specific gravity is the ratio of the weight of a certain volume of a given substance to the weight of an equal volume of water. Did you know that, by definition, 1 litre of water weighs 1 kilogram? Anything lighter has a lower specific gravity and anything heavier has a higher specific gravity. For example, milk has a specific gravity that is slightly higher than water while petrol has a specific gravity that's less than water.

Using the principle that is now named after him, Archimedes was able to find out the specific gravities of different bodies. His method has been used for centuries to judge the composition of objects. For example, in mining, it is used to calculate how much mineral – like gold or iron ore – a rock contains. Similarly, in construction, specific gravity can help determine whether the ground can handle the weight of the building.

## Simple Numbers

The distance around a circle is called the circumference. The distance across a circle is called the diameter. Pi (π) is the ratio of the circumference of a circle to its diameter. The size of the circle is unimportant. It doesn't matter whether the circle is big or small. The ratio is always pi. Archimedes calculated pi to the most precise value known at that time. Using geometric methods, he was able to show that the value of pi was between 22/7 and 223/71. Archimedes also found, and mathematically proved, the formulas to calculate the volume and surface area of a sphere. These are formulas, which we take for granted today, form the basis of a lot of the technologies that make our lives comfortable.

Archimedes was the first person to apply the results of physics to solve problems in pure mathematics. His discoveries would go on to inspire Galileo and Newton to investigate motion and find the mathematics behind it.

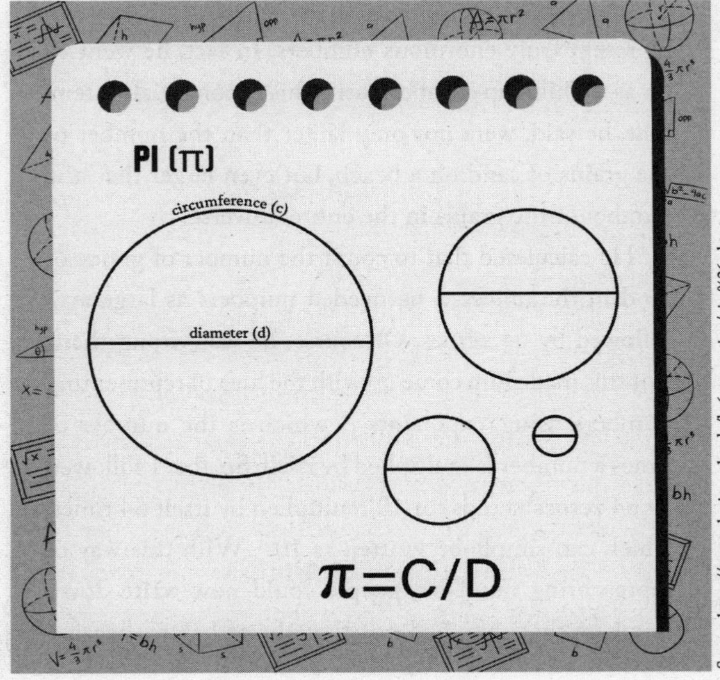


Source: https://www.physics.ucla.edu/k-6connection/pi,p%26p.htm

## Archimedes, Exponents and Google

Archimedes did something that changed mathematics forever.

The story goes that Archimedes got tired of people saying that no one could count the number of grains of sand on a beach. *And the largest number the Greeks could write down at that time was 10,000! They just called bigger numbers 'myriad' and gave up.*

So, Archimedes thought up a new system that could represent truly enormous numbers. In fact, he went so far as to think up numbers, using his exponential system, that, he said, were not only larger than the number of the grains of sand on a beach, but even larger than the number of the grains in the entire universe.

He calculated that to count the number of grains of sand in the universe, he needed numbers as large as 1 followed by 64 zeroes. Of course, he was wrong there. But this made him come up with the idea of representing numbers using 'exponents' – which is the number of times a number is multiplied by itself. So, the '1 followed by 64 zeroes' stands for 10 multiplied by itself 64 times, which can simply be written as $10^{64}$. With this way of representing numbers, people could now write down numbers that they had not thought of before, because they were simply too large. For example, 'Googol' is the term used to represent the number 1 followed by 100 zeroes. It can be simply written as $10^{100}$, where the 100 is called the 'exponent'.

Of course, Archimedes's $10^{64}$ didn't look like $10^{64}$ at all, because the Greeks had not discovered zero and used letters of their alphabets to represent numbers. So $10^{64}$ would have looked quite ugly by today's standards.

Did you know that when entrepreneurs Larry Page and Sergei Brin decided to set up their company, they wanted to name it after $10^{100}$? But when they were filling up the form to register the name, they spelt the word wrong. And that's how we ended up with Google, instead of Googol.

## A Sad End

Archimedes' fame had spread far and wide during his lifetime. Yet, his death was tragic. In 212 BCE, during what is now called the Second Punic war, Roman forces under General Marcus Claudius Marcellus captured the city of Syracuse after a two-year-long siege. Their original attack by sea had failed due to Archimedes' inventions.

The physicist was studying a mathematical diagram he had drawn on the floor of his courtyard when a Roman soldier arrived and commanded him to accompany him and meet General Marcellus. Archimedes, deep in thought, told the soldier to step back and not disturb his diagram. The soldier was enraged and killed the 75-year-old genius. Marcellus was extremely angry about this, because he had heard a lot about Archimedes and had specifically ordered that he should not be harmed.

And that's how the world lost one of its finest scientific minds ever.

# 4

# Aryabhata the Genius

Indian mathematicians who lived around 1,700 to 1,000 years ago discovered things that brilliant European physicists would only figure out hundreds of years later. They made huge advances in algebra, geometry, trigonometry, even invented the higher mathematics field of calculus 600 years before Newton and Gottfried Wilhelm Leibniz developed it on their own. They then used their theories to make astronomical predictions, many of which have now been proven to be extremely accurate.

Indian mathematical knowledge reached Arabia through traders who travelled frequently between the two regions, and then spread from Arabia to Europe. Perhaps the greatest of Indian mathematicians was

Source: Atlas Obscura

*The Aryabhata statue at the Inter-University Centre for Astronomy and Astrophysics, Pune. (We don't know what he really looked like. This was the sculptor's conception.)*

Aryabhata. When India launched its first satellite in space in 1975, it was named after him.

## We Know So Little about Him

Aryabhata was an astonishing genius who lived in the fifth and sixth centuries during the great Gupta Empire, considered a Golden Age of Indian arts, culture and science. During this age, impressive monuments were built; literature flourished; Kalidasa, the greatest-ever Sanskrit poet, and Charaka and Sushruta, two of the greatest doctors, lived during this period. Nalanda, at the time the world's largest university, was also established, and mathematics and science made huge strides forward.

While there is no agreement among scholars about the region of India Aryabhata came from, there is consensus that he likely completed his higher studies and much of his research in Pataliputra – now Patna – which was then the largest city in India. Some historians believe that he may also have been the head of Nalanda University, which was not very far from Pataliputra.

Sadly, much of his original works have been lost, but we still know something about his achievements through the few that have survived, the accounts of his students and Arabic translations of his Sanskrit books.

## Geometry and Algebra

Aryabhata's most important book – *Aryabhatiya* – has thankfully survived. Following the tradition of those times, it is written in verse form. Although it is a short book with only 108 verses (not including the 13 verses that introduce the reader to what he was attempting), it covers an amazing number of areas, from algebra to astrophysics.

For instance, he writes: 'Add 4 to 100 [that's 104], multiply by 8 [that's 832], and then add 62,000 [giving us 62,832]. By this rule, the circumference of a circle with a diameter of 20,000 can be approached.' This implies that for a circle whose diameter is 20,000 (this is a radius of 10,000), the circumference will be 62,832. Now if we divide 62,832 by 20,000, this gives us 3.1416, which is the value of pi correct to the third decimal place.*

Aryabhata used the word 'approached' for pi, instead of something like 'calculated'. This suggests that he knew that pi is an 'irrational number' – a number that can never be expressed absolutely correctly as a fraction. For instance, a number like 1.5 can be expressed perfectly as the fraction 3/2. But pi can only be represented approximately as a fraction – 22/7, the one we all learnt in school. And Aryabhata worked this out 1,300 years before the French mathematician Johann Heinrich Lambert actually proved that pi is irrational.

It is possible that some of this work had been done earlier by Indian mathematicians, maybe even centuries before Aryabhata. But it was he who refined them, simplified them, added his insights and put them all together in a logical format.

---

* Rounding off in the fourth decimal, since we now know $\pi$ to five decimals is 3.14159.

## How Large Is Pi?

Pi is an irrational number. It never ends in a pattern, so you never know what's coming next. Suppose you divide 20 by 3. You will get 6.6666 . . . till infinity. That's boring. But pi goes on and on and keeps surprising you. You can never pin it down.

Now that we have very powerful computers, people have used them to calculate pi to more than a million decimal places.

Here's pi up to 500 decimal places:

3.14159265358979323846264338327950288419716939937510582097494459230781640628620899628034825342117067982148086513282306647093844609550582231725359408128481117450284102701938521105559644622948954930381964428810975665933446128475648233786783165271201909145648566923460348610454326648213393607260249141273724587006606315588174881520920962829254091715364367892590360011330530548820466521384146951941511609433057270365759591953092186117381932611793105118548074462379962749567351885752724891227938183011949129

Of the 108 verses in Aryabhata's book, 34 cover topics that we are now taught in arithmetic, algebra and geometry in middle and high school. For instance, there are simple, quadratic and simultaneous equations, and mensuration – the part of geometry that helps us to calculate lengths, areas and volumes. He also told us how to calculate square and cube roots.

In just one verse, he told us how to calculate sine values. The sine is an important ratio in trigonometry – the study of triangles. Sine is the ratio of the length of the side opposite one of the angles in a right-angled triangle to the length of the longest side. It is one of the most basic values on which much of our modern physics and engineering is based, and it is crucial when it comes to building flyovers or calculating the paths of rockets going to Mars.

Aryabhata called sine 'ardha-jya', which means 'half-chord'. For simplicity, people started calling it '*jya*'. When his work reached the Arab countries, translators found this difficult, since in Arabic writings, vowels are omitted. So they just wrote 'jb'. It came to be pronounced as '*jaib*'. But that word meant 'pocket' – in north India, people still use that word for 'pocket'. In the twelfth century, 600 years after Aryabhata's work, when the Italian Gerardo of Cremona translated these writings from Arabic into Latin, he called it 'sinus', which is the Latin for 'pocket'. And that's why we call it 'sine' now!

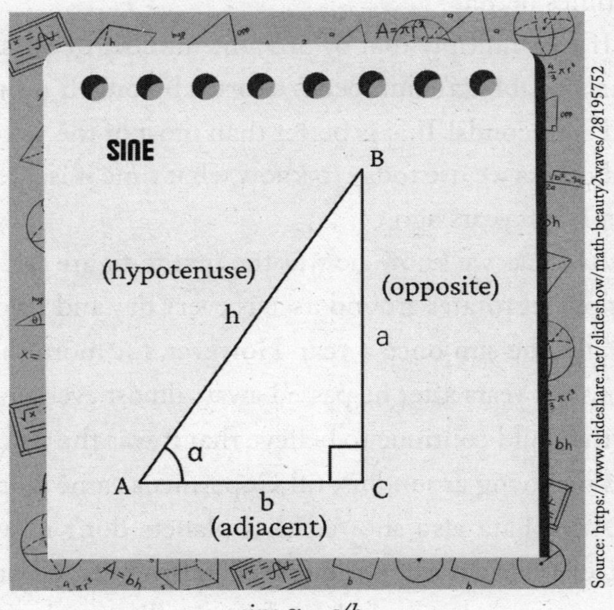


*sine* $\alpha = a/h$

## The Planets and Years

Aryabhata devoted the rest of his book to some amazing discoveries in astronomy. He had studied how stars in the night sky change positions as time goes by. Based on what he saw, he calculated the length of a day. If we convert his findings into today's units, he had worked out that a day is **23 hours, 56 minutes and 4.1 seconds** long. This is off by just 0.01 second from the number we have now, with scientific equipment that is thousands of times better!

If you multiply that by 365, the number of days in a year, Aryabhata's number is shorter by only 3 minutes and 20 seconds! That is better than most of the watches and clocks we use today to know what time it is. He did this 1,600 years ago.

As far as we know, he was the first to figure out that our planet rotates around its axis every day and revolves around the sun once a year. However, for more than a thousand years after he passed away, almost everyone on earth would continue to believe that it was the sun that was revolving around us, till Copernicus came along.

Aryabhata also showed that planets don't move in circles around the sun and that their orbits are elliptical, that is, somewhat oval-shaped. So the distance between the sun and the earth changes over a year. The earth is closest to the sun in mid-July – the height of summer in much of the northern hemisphere – and farthest in January – winter.

Today, all of us know that the moon and the planets produce no light of their own. We see them because they reflect sunlight. Guess who the first person was to discover this? That's right – Aryabhata. He said that a lunar eclipse takes place when the earth comes between the sun and the moon and its shadow falls on the moon, turning it all dark. He did detailed calculations to show why sometimes we see only partial eclipses of the moon. When the sun, the earth and the moon are in such positions in relation to one another that the earth's shadow covers only a part of the moon, we have a partial eclipse. A full lunar eclipse happens when the earth is directly in line between the sun and the moon, and its shadow covers the whole moon.

Other Indian astronomers who came after him improved on Aryabhata's astronomical calculations. When the eighteenth-century Italian scientist Guillaume Le Gentil visited India, he was amazed to see that the Indian estimates of how long the lunar eclipse of 30 August 1765 would last were off by only 41 seconds!

Aryabhata's calculations were also used to fix the Hindu calendar. Arab and Persian mathematicians studied his work, improved upon it with further observations, and developed their own calendar in the eleventh century. That calendar, called Jalali, is still followed in countries like Iran.

## One of the Greatest Physicists Ever

It may not be too wrong to say that Aryabhata was as great a scientist as Newton or Einstein. And remember, he had no telescopes, no modern equipment. He could only use his eyes to study the skies. He had to create much of the math that he used to understand how the universe worked. Sadly, his work reached Europe only through Arabic translations, so his achievements were seen as the achievements of Arabs, even though Arab mathematicians acknowledged in their books that they were only building on the work that Aryabhata had done. Aryabhata's work was also refined by other Indian mathematicians such as Brahmagupta, Bhaskara and Madhava.

Today, we cannot say with any certainty who Aryabhata's parents were, whether he had children, how long he lived, where he died, or what he looked like. But to commemorate his many achievements, we have built statues of him, to remember and honour him.

## Who Invented Algebra?

All of us have had to study algebra in school, and some of us may even have dreaded it. The word 'algebra' is derived from the Arabic term 'al-jabr', which means 'reunion of broken parts', from the title of a ninth-century math book by the Persian mathematician and astronomer al-Khwarizmi. He used 'al-jabr' to refer to moving a term from one side of an equation to the other and balancing the equation.

Al-Khwarizmi's book was a translation of Aryabhata's work with some of his own additions, and the Persian acknowledged this. Aryabhata had invented the rules for simple, quadratic and simultaneous equations, which form the foundations of algebra. He also worked out a way of solving indeterminate equations (equations that can have many solutions), which had baffled mathematicians for ages.

In his book, al-Khwarizmi cites many of Aryabhata's discoveries. In fact, the term 'al-jabr' itself could very well be a reference or translation of the Sanskrit term for what we today call 'algebra' – 'kuttaka', which means 'breaking into small parts'.

When Al-Khwarizmi's book was translated into Latin, 'al-jabr' became 'algebra'.

# 5

# From Zero to Infinity

What is the first thing we learn in mathematics? We learn counting and writing down numbers. The decimal system of numbers is easy to learn and so convenient that with the help of just nine numerals and zero, we can build any number and go as high as we want to. But this method was not known to the ancients. In the olden times, people used symbols, tokens, marks on clay tablets and so on to denote numbers. It was all very cumbersome.

## Bhaskara I's Wheel

Bhaskara I was a seventh-century CE Indian mathematician and astronomer. He is called Bhaskara I to differentiate him from Bhaskara II, who was a twelfth-century mathematician. Bhaskara I introduced the decimal number system that we use today and was the first in the world to use a circle to denote zero. The Western world adopted this system 900 years later, in the sixteenth century.

Like Aryabhata, very little is known about Bhaskara I's life. He possibly lived in Vallabhi, Saurashtra, which is located in present-day Gujarat. Bhaskara I studied the book *Aryabhatiya* in great detail. In fact, it is quite likely that it was he who named the book. He did original research on 33 verses of the book, which dealt with variable equations and trigonometric formulae. Without Bhaskara I, all of Aryabhata's work may have been lost.

While Aryabhata had not bothered to provide proofs of his findings, presenting them as truths instead, Bhaskara I was different. He insisted on proving mathematical rules rigorously and writing them down for others to know. Bhaskara I took forward Aryabhata's work by developing an approximate formula for calculating sine values. He also established relations between sine and cosine – like the sine, the cosine function is a trigonometric ratio – and also worked out a method to calculate the values of sine for a large number of angles. He may have invented this method, which we now call 'interpolation', something that Newton worked out independently a thousand years later. Bhaskara I is also credited as the first mathematician to work on quadrilaterals – four-sided geometric figures including squares and rectangles – with unequal non-parallel sides.

## How Bhaskara I Changed the World

Bhaskara I did not invent the decimal number system, but he was the first person to make it simple enough for everyone to understand and use.

Before his work, numbers were written in words or allegories and usually arranged in verses. For example, the number 1 was 'moon', since there is only one moon in our sky. The number 2 was represented by wings or eyes because these always occur in pairs. Obviously, this made calculations quite difficult for most people, and utterly impossible for those who did not have a certain level of formal education.

While India already had a system that did not need anyone to write words or draw pictures to represent numbers, before Bhaskara I, it was not being used much. This system was called the 'Brahmi' number system and had existed for at least 800 years. Brahmi used simple symbols, similar to what we use today. After all, a '1' or a '7' or a '9' is just a symbol created by the stroke of a pencil or the tap of a keyboard. Bhaskara I took the nine number symbols of the Brahmi system and then just drew **a small circle** after them. This was the invention of zero.

Before this invention by Bhaskara I, people had to be highly educated to know what actual number a writer was referring to – was it 20 or 200? With the circle-shaped zero, the problem was now solved. One could just write a 2 and add one or two circles – zeroes – after it and everyone knew what the number was!

Thus, Bhaskara I changed the world and improved human life just as much as the unknown person who had invented the wheel thousands of years ago. One interesting thing, of course, is that the zero is a circle, just like the wheel!

Bhaskara I was also an astronomer, who did pioneering work on the movements of planets, phases of the moon, and solar and lunar eclipses. We had mentioned in the last chapter that the first space satellite that India launched was named Aryabhata. Well, the second one was named Bhaskara.

## Prime Numbers

As we have seen before – and we will see more of this – many discoveries of the early Indian mathematicians spread to the West through the Arabs, so they were seen as Arab mathematics. Many of the theorems that were formulated in India ages ago are now known by European names, because European mathematicians, unaware that these proofs had been worked out many centuries before in another part of the world, discovered them through Arabic translations.

Prime numbers are a fascinating set of numbers. A prime number can be divided only by 1 and itself – such as 7, 13, 23, 37. The largest prime number known till now is $2^{82,589,933} - 1$, a number that has 24,862,048 digits when written using the decimal system. An important rule about prime numbers that Bhaskara I first discovered and proved is now known as Wilson's Theorem, after John Wilson, a British mathematician from the eighteenth century. Bhaskara I's theorems about the solutions to equations are today known as Pell's Equations, after yet another British mathematician of the seventeenth century, John Pell. Both Wilson's Theorem and Pell's Equations are very high-level math, difficult to explain to anyone who is not doing a college course in number theory – about how numbers behave.

## Brahmagupta's Negatives and Positive Numbers

Brahmagupta, who lived in the seventh century, was another great Indian mathematician whom we should be proud of. He may have been just two years older than Bhaskara, and they seem to have passed away in the same year. He made many advances in astronomy and number systems and invented methods for finding square roots of numbers and solving quadratic equations. These are basic mathematical rules that all schools now teach.

Again, like Aryabhata and Bhaskara I, we do not know much about Brahmagupta's life. He wrote two important works on mathematics and astronomy. The first was a text named *Brahmasphutasiddhanta* (The Proved Doctrines of Brahma), which he finished in 628 CE at Bhillamala, the capital of the land ruled by the Gurjara dynasty in present-day Rajasthan. This text consists of 25 chapters, covering various topics in mathematics and mathematical astronomy. His second work was *Khandkhadyaka* (Edible Bits), which has eight chapters on mathematical astronomy.

Brahmagupta thought deeply about the number zero. In the *Brahmasphutasiddhanta*, he gave a very good definition of this number. He said that we obtain zero when we subtract a number from itself. 'When zero is added to a number or subtracted from a number, the number remains unchanged; and a number multiplied by zero becomes zero.' This may seem very obvious to even a child today, but it was a great step forward at that time. No one before Brahmagupta had put it so simply.

However, he also said that zero divided by zero is zero, which was later shown to be wrong. The correct answer is 'undefined' – we cannot state it under the rules of mathematics. This is a complex concept, but let's try to put it as simply as we can. Suppose 5x=40, where x is a non-zero number. To know what x is, we simply need to divide 40 by 5. But if 0x=0, x can be anything at all – 11 or 49 or 16,245. There's no way for us to know what that number being multiplied was. So multiplying by 0 is a 'non-invertible operation'. And dividing 0 by 0 is just mathematically meaningless.

In the *Brahmasphutasiddhanta*, Brahmagupta gave important formulas to calculate the area of a cyclic quadrilateral, and the length of the diagonals. A cyclic quadrilateral is a four-sided figure inscribed in a circle.

Later in life, Brahmagupta moved to Ujjain to head the astronomical observatory there – at that time the most advanced observatory in the country. Brilliant mathematicians like Varahamihira had worked there and built a strong school of mathematical astronomy.

George Sarton, the Belgian-American chemist who is regarded as the founder of the study of the history of science as a special field, called Brahmagupta 'one of the greatest scientists of his race and the greatest of his time'.

### From Brahmagupta to Algorithm

Some hundred years or so after Brahmagupta's death, his works reached the Turkish court of Caliph Al-Mansur, apparently through an astrologer from Sindh called Kanaka. His two texts *Brahmasphutasiddhanta* and *Khandkhadyaka* were soon translated into Arabic under the titles *Sindhind* and *Arakhan*. Over the next few years, the decimal number system spread around the Arab world.

In the ninth century, the Persian mathematician Al-Khwarizmi wrote a text called *Kitāb al-Hisāb al-Hindī* (Book of Indian Computation) based on Brahmagupta's books. Yes, here he is again, Al-Khwarizmi, the man who took Aryabhata's discoveries to the world! We must remember that Al-Khwarizmi did not seek undue credit and clearly stated that he was writing about Indian math. However, Europeans did not pay any attention to this.

In the twelfth century, this book was translated into Latin as *Algorismi De Numero Indorum* (Algorismi on Indian Numbers) by the English scientist Abelard of Bath. 'Al-Khwarizmi' was a name impossible to write correctly in Latin. Just as the British wrote 'Thiruvananthapuram' as 'Trivandrum' and 'Vadodara' as 'Baroda', Abelard wrote the Persian's name as 'Algorismi'. It was through this book that Brahmagupta's decimal number system reached Europe and then spread across the planet.

Some years later, the French scholar Alexander of Villedieu wrote a Latin text called *Carmen de Algorismo* (The Song of Algorismo). The first line of the book was: 'Algorism is the art by which we use those Indian figures, which number two times five.' Two times five is of course ten, which is the basis of the decimal system. The English turned 'algorism' into 'algorithm', meaning a set of rules that precisely defines the steps to do something or solve a problem.

So Al-Khwarizmi's work gives us two of the most famous mathematical terms in the world: algebra and algorithms. All computer science is based on algorithms. In fact, even everyday tasks like tying shoelaces or frying an egg can be broken down into step-by-step instructions – essentially, algorithms!

## Infinity and Calculus

The great mathematician and astronomer Madhava lived in Kerala during the late fourteenth and early fifteenth century. He is regarded as the founder of the Kerala School of Mathematics and Astronomy, which flourished between the fourteenth and sixteenth centuries and produced many brilliant scholars.

The Kerala School focused on solving astronomical problems and discovered many mathematical concepts. Notably, it made original contributions to the fields of infinite series and calculus.

What is an infinite series?

Let's say we have a never-ending sequence of numbers like this:

½, ¼, ⅛, ¹⁄₁₆ and on and on and on.

Here, each number is half of the one that came before it. Now you add all these numbers up. How can one possibly do that? After all, you can't even imagine how small the number can get, because there is no smallest number! Madhava solved this problem. He developed a formula by which you can know what all these numbers will add up to.

For example, the sum of this sequence, where every number is half the previous one, ½ + ¼ + ⅛ + ¹⁄₁₆ . . .

is 1. The sum of this sequence, where every number is ¼th of the previous number: $\frac{1}{4} + \frac{1}{16} + \frac{1}{64} + \frac{1}{256} \ldots$ is $\frac{1}{3}$.

There are also infinite sums that cannot be added up to any finite number, since they just keep growing larger and larger. For example, the series $1 + \frac{1}{2} + \frac{1}{3} + \frac{1}{4} \ldots$ is the famous harmonic series in which each number is generated by dividing 1 successively by 1, 2, 3, 4 and so on. This series can't be calculated; it just keeps growing. The Kerala School worked out methods for judging which series can be calculated and which cannot.

We won't go into the details of how all this is worked out, because it involves somewhat higher-level concepts like 'limit' and 'convergence'. Infinite series formulas have great value in developing theories in mathematics and physics, and they also help us in very practical ways in many diverse areas.

When a company makes a world-class football, the people making it may not even know it, but the design and specifications of the ball are based on an infinite series of calculations. The designer needs to know how long it will take for a bouncing ball to stop bouncing and come to a rest.

When someone sings a song and records it or takes a photo, the original files are very heavy. Infinite series mathematics is used to compress that song or photo file – and the result is a much smaller file. This is not perfectly the same as the original sound or image, but it is so extremely similar that hardly anyone will ever know the difference. This new file can be mailed, posted and downloaded very easily. So next time you download an **.mp3 or .jpeg**, you should thank Madhava and his students!

Madhava's work formed the basis of calculus, which was developed as a branch of mathematics two centuries later in Europe by Newton and Leibniz. We talk about them in Chapter 8. It was only in the early nineteenth century that Westerners began to recognize the contributions made by the Kerala School. Without calculus, our lives would be very different. We would not have been able to build safe bridges and efficient mobile phone networks, study how diseases spread, or send rockets to Mars. In fact, without calculus, we would not even be able to work out how gravity works or know how to calculate its effects!

Madhava lived in modern-day Irinjalakuda in Kerala. He started what is known as the '*guru parampara*' or the 'chain of teachers' in the Kerala School – a tradition in which a guru must teach his students in such a way that the best of them become gurus in turn and continue the search, preservation and imparting of knowledge over many generations. Sadly, most of Madhava's work has been lost over time. We know about the great discoveries that he made from the references and commentaries by his successors in their works.

Madhava was referred to as *'Gol Vid'* or 'one who knows the sphere'. This title proves that Indian mathematicians and astronomers knew that the earth is a sphere and developed their theories based on this much before the West accepted this fact. Kim Plofker, the author of the book *Mathematics in India* (2008), described Madhava's work as the 'crest jewel' of the Kerala School.

6

# How Copernicus Shifted the Centre of the Universe

When you get away from polluted cities and gaze at the night sky, it looks vast and full of stars – too many to be counted. People have always looked up and wondered about their place in the universe. Today, we know that our universe started with a Big Bang about 14 billion years ago and has been expanding ever since, though scientists are still refining the details of this theory as instruments such as the amazingly powerful James Webb Telescope throw up new data. The universe doesn't have a centre. It doesn't have an edge either. However, back when there were no telescopes and other sophisticated instruments, people assumed that the earth was the centre of the universe.

Two observations supported this idea. First, to every person living on earth, the sun seems to revolve around it once per day. The moon and the planets also have their own orbits of motion. At the same time, they also appear to revolve around the earth once each day. Even the stars seem to be revolving around the earth. Second, the earth appears stationary to us (even though it's actually moving and spinning at a great speed). Given these two observations, it seemed obvious to the ancients that the earth was the centre of the universe.

In the third century BCE, the Greek mathematician and astronomer, Aristarchus of Samos, was the first to suggest that the earth is a sphere and that the sun, not the earth, is the centre of the solar system. But in his lifetime, people thought his theories were the ravings of a madman.

Unlike those of Aryabhata, some of Aristarchus' calculations have turned out to be wildly incorrect. After observing the sun and the moon for a long time, he concluded, using geometry, that the distance between the earth and the sun was 19 times more than the distance between the earth and the moon. The actual distance is 390 times. His geometric logic was correct, but his conclusions were wrong.

Aristarchus' theories went against what the great

philosopher Aristotle had believed and also contradicted the theories of the later Greek astronomer, Claudius Ptolemy. This was a very important reason why his theories were ignored. Aristotle had passed away when Aristarchus was still a child, but he was held in such high esteem in society that it was assumed that anyone saying anything different was wrong. How dare they not agree with Aristotle?

The book that Aristarchus wrote, explaining his logic and conclusions, was also lost. We know of his theories only because Archimedes had read it and written about it in one of his own books.

## Elementary

Aristotle said that there were four fundamental elements – fire, air, water and earth – and all of space was filled with a combination of these elements. Each of these four elements had a specific 'weight'. Earth was the heaviest, water was lighter, air and fire were the lightest. Aristotle believed that the lighter substances drifted away from the centre of the universe and the heavier ones gravitated towards the centre, where the earth was located.

According to him, there were seven planets, which

were known as wandering stars because they moved through the zodiac signs in addition to travelling around the earth. The sun and the moon were two of these wandering stars! Beyond that, there were the fixed stars. The four elements moved vertically, the heavier ones moving towards the earth and the lighter ones floating away. The celestial bodies were made of a fifth element or 'quintessence', which moved in perfect circles around the earth, completing a rotation each day. All this is, of course, very far from the truth that we know today. However, people believed in his theory because Aristotle was highly regarded as a thinker. Philosophy and physics were seen as the same thing in his time, and experimental verification of a hypothesis wasn't considered that important.

## The Centre of the Universe

In the second century CE, Claudius Ptolemy, an astronomer based in Alexandria, created a new model of the universe, based on observations made with his naked eye. But in his model, too, the earth was the centre of the universe.

His idea was that all the heavenly bodies were attached to **crystal spheres**, which revolved around the earth. The moon was on the innermost sphere. The planets were attached to two spheres. One sphere was centred a little away from the earth and the other was fixed inside the first sphere.

Ptolemy's greatest work was *The Almagest*. This was a collection of all the astronomical knowledge of Greece, to which he had made valuable contributions. The information and the concepts contained in *The Almagest* were so complete that nobody in the West added anything to them for more than a thousand years, and people continued to believe that the earth was the centre of the universe. Of course, only very few scholars in Europe were aware of Aryabhata's work, and those who were, appeared to have focused on his mathematics rather than his astronomy. As we will see, this also had to do with religious faith.

## Renaissance Man

Nicolaus Copernicus was a Polish astronomer who lived in the fifteenth–sixteenth centuries. His Heliocentric Theory launched modern astronomy and set off the 'Scientific Revolution', which would replace the Greek view of the universe that had reigned for nearly 2,000 years in Europe.

Copernicus was a perfect example of the Renaissance Man – a well-educated person who excelled in a wide variety of fields. It was during the Renaissance – a French word for 'rebirth' – lasting from the fourteenth century to the seventeenth century, that Europe emerged from what is called the Dark Ages, a time period that spanned several hundred years when thought and science stagnated.

During the Renaissance, European scholars rediscovered Greek and Roman knowledge. Educated Europeans came to believe that humans were limitless in their capacity to think and should be open to all types of knowledge.

Copernicus was a mathematician, astronomer, physician, economist, legal expert, translator, artist and a whole lot of other things. He studied mathematics and logic at the University of Krakow in Poland, and law and medicine in Italy. This indicates his wide range of interests. He also spoke five languages.

Unlike most of his fellow students, he questioned what he was taught at the universities. He was unable to accept Aristotle's view of the universe and Ptolemy's use of a complicated system of spheres to explain the motion of the heavenly bodies.

At the age of 30, Copernicus came back to Poland to

live with his uncle as his secretary and physician. This gave him free time to make astronomical observations. Telescopes had not yet been invented so he studied the night sky with devices that looked like long wooden measuring rods joined together. These helped him measure the angles between distant bodies in the sky and how they moved.

In 1514, Copernicus presented his Heliocentric Theory to some of his friends who were interested in astronomy. He confidently stated that the earth rotates about its axis and revolves around the sun. It was a short report and did not include any mathematical calculations because he wanted to keep things simple. He collected more data and worked on a detailed manuscript.

But he was fearful that if he made his findings public, he would get into trouble because his theories seemed to refute a few passages in the Old Testament, such as Joshua 10, in which Joshua, the leader of the Jewish tribes, is said to have stopped the sun in the sky; and 2 Kings 20, where Hezekiah, king of Judah, got the sun to reverse its 'orbit' around the earth by a few degrees. Copernicus sent his book *On the Revolutions of Celestial Orbs* for publication only in 1543, when he believed that he would die soon. It is said that he received the first printed copies of his book on his deathbed, looked at them and passed away the next day.

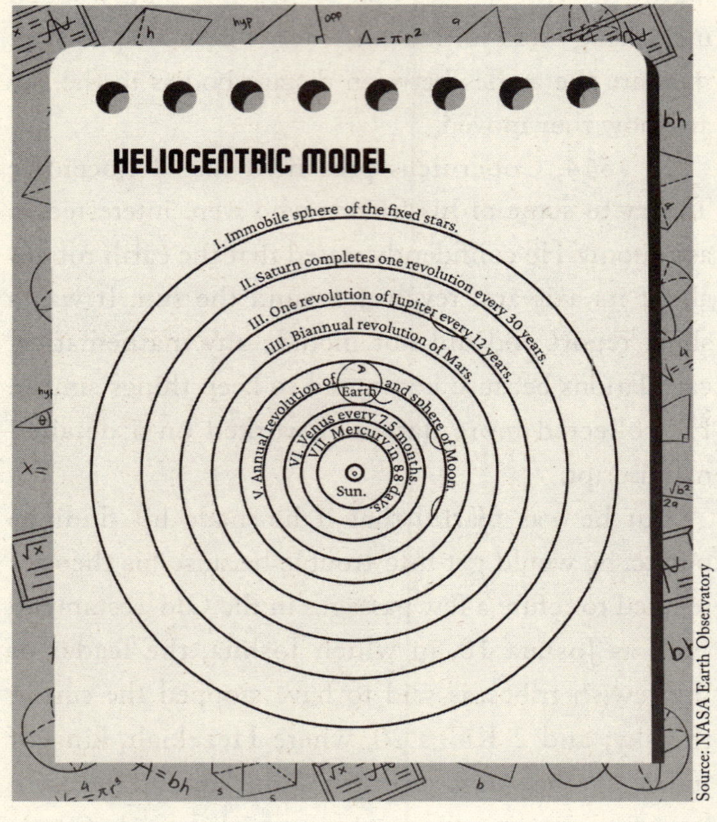


*Engraving from Nicholas Copernicus's* De revolutionibus orbium coelestium (On the Revolutions of Celestial Orbs), *which illustrates his observations about the planets and the solar system*

What is interesting, however, is that the Catholic Church paid little attention to the book. *Revolutions* hardly sold because it was so technical and difficult that only expert astronomers could understand it. It was only in 1616, 73 years after Copernicus's death, that the Church banned it. **The ban** wouldn't be lifted until two centuries later in 1835.

## Rotation and Revolution

These are the conclusions that Copernicus reached:

- The earth is not the centre of the universe.
- The sun is fixed and is the centre of the universe. Copernicus held on to Ptolemy's idea of crystal spheres and said that the earth and other planets revolve around the sun in perfectly circular orbits inside the spheres.
- The earth rotates about its axis and revolves around the sun.
- The stars are fixed but appear to be moving because of the earth's movement across the sky.

Some of these ideas are not correct. The sun is roughly at the centre of the solar system but certainly not the universe. The orbits of the planets are elliptical and not circular. There are no crystal spheres; the stars

*The Dreistab is an instrument that Copernicus built to study the skies and determine the altitude of heavenly bodies.*

are not stationary. However, Copernicus' ideas were revolutionary at that time and completely changed the way later scientists viewed the world.

The Heliocentric Theory was the foundation on which Galileo and Newton developed physics further. Over time, people started recording observations that supported the heliocentric idea of the solar system, as opposed to the 'geocentric' idea, which puts earth at the centre of the universe. In 1610, with the help of his telescope, Galileo saw moons orbiting Jupiter. This clearly disproved Aristotle's view that everything orbits around the earth. Later, German mathematician Johannes Kepler formulated a series of laws that described the orbits of planets around the sun. Newton built on these laws to explain why planets moved the way they did and introduced the concept of gravity. All these are extremely important milestones in the story of physics.

# 7

# Galileo Galilei: The Father of Modern Science

Galileo Galilei (1564–1642) is a towering figure in the story of physics. He is known as the father of modern science. He not only discovered some of the basic rules of physics but also created some of the principles of good scientific research. Even today, scientists follow these methods.

Like Copernicus, Galileo was a man of many interests. He was an expert musician who played several instruments. He had a great deal of artistic talent and even considered a career as a painter. He was sent to the University of Pisa to study medicine, but soon decided that it was mathematics that really interested him. However, due to some financial troubles in the family, he could not complete his education and decided to study mathematics on his own. Some years later, he would return to the university as a professor of mathematics, even though he did not have a college degree.

His first famous experiment was about gravity. He climbed to the top of the Leaning Tower of Pisa and dropped two metal spheres of different weights, observing that both hit the ground at the same time. Thus, he disproved Aristotle's hypothesis that heavy objects fall faster than light ones and concluded that all falling bodies have the same acceleration. He also deduced correctly that when an object takes more time to fall, it is because of air resistance.

In fact, later scientists have been able to demonstrate

that in the absence of air resistance in a vacuum, a feather and a football would fall at the same rate.

## The Night Sky

Galileo had a quality that all great scientists have: a curious and questioning mind. At the age of 20, when he was still a student, he observed a lamp swinging back and forth from a cathedral ceiling. Something prompted him to measure the time the lamp took to complete one oscillation.

There were no wristwatches then, so Galileo used his pulse to measure the time. He made the remarkable discovery that the time the lamp took to complete one oscillation was exactly the same, no matter how big the swing was. This discovery came to be known as the **'law of the pendulum'**, and it has been used ever since in the construction of clocks.

In 1609, Galileo heard about a device that had been invented in the Netherlands, which allowed people to see faraway things up close. This was of course the telescope, and it was being used mainly as a fun item for visitors to fairs. People paid money to look at distant objects through it.

But Galileo understood how a telescope could be

much more useful. So he built his own, which was far more powerful, and became the first person on earth to turn a telescope towards the night sky and study the heavens.

## 'And Yet It Moves'

Galileo discovered that the surface of the moon is not flat but riddled with craters. He observed that there are many more stars than those that can be seen through the naked eye. He also discovered the moons that orbited around Jupiter. This was direct proof of Copernicus' theory that the sun and not the earth, was at the centre of the universe.

In 1632, Galileo published a book in support of this theory. The claims made in the book were bolder than the ones made by Copernicus. Unfortunately, this was a time when there was much bitterness between Protestants and Catholics, and the Catholic Church had become very sensitive about people defying its authority. The Church felt threatened because Galileo's hypotheses went against their teachings about the earth being stationary and the sun revolving around the earth.

Galileo, a devout Christian, argued that his ideas did not oppose religious truth. He said that his work was about 'how the heavens go' whereas the Church taught people 'how to go to heaven'! But the Church charged Galileo with 'heresy' – the crime of believing that the Bible and the Church were wrong, punishable by death. To save his life, Galileo agreed to withdraw his book and take back his opinion that the earth moves around the sun. But the Church still decided that he was too dangerous a man to be allowed to move around freely and sentenced him to house arrest for the rest of his life. He spent the last ten years of his life unable to leave his home.

It is said that as Galileo was dying, the last words he spoke to his daughter who was sitting by his bed were, 'And yet it moves.' He had been forced to announce in public that his theories were wrong, but in his heart of hearts, he knew he was right. The earth revolved round the sun.

**In 1992, 350 years after** Galileo passed away, the Church finally admitted that it was wrong to have persecuted Galileo.

The discoveries of Copernicus and Galileo led to the Scientific Revolution. Beginning in the 1600s, many curious people began to carefully observe nature. They questioned what Aristotle and other ancient scholars had said and what the Bible proclaimed. These early scientists gathered data, put forth hypotheses, performed experiments and drew conclusions. Science flourished, and important discoveries were made.

The Special Theory of Relativity, which Einstein proposed in 1905, has far-reaching consequences. But its basic assumption was first stated by Galileo Galilei in 1632. We will read more about this in a later chapter.

**The Math of the Universe**

Galileo was the first person to make mathematics an essential part of the study of natural phenomena. Before Galileo, natural phenomena were studied in a qualitative way – without the use of any math. Even Copernicus did not use math in his description of the heliocentric universe.

The book of nature, Galileo held, is written in mathematical language and that 'its characters are triangles, circles and other geometrical figures, without which it is humanly impossible to understand a single word of it; without these, one wanders about in a dark labyrinth'. In *Discorsi* (Discourses), he succeeded in providing proof that nature is describable using math.

Galileo was the first person to use mathematical

formulas to express his findings. Then he used these formulas to make further predictions and finally he performed experiments to verify his predictions. This is known as the 'scientific method'.

Newton followed the same approach when framing the fundamental laws of physics. These developments led to the Industrial Revolution and changed the course of human history.

# 8

# How Newton Uncovered the Laws of Nature

Galileo's work set the stage for Sir Isaac Newton (1642–1727) to discover the laws that govern motion. It was a remarkable feat. Newton managed to explain all the observations made till then with the help of his theory of gravity and three elegant laws.

## Who Cares for Exams?

Newton's life was very interesting. His father, also named Isaac Newton, passed away three months before he was born. At the time of birth, he was such a tiny baby that he was not expected to live. But he did. In school, he did not do particularly well in his exams, and when he was 16, his mother ordered him to quit classrooms and become a farmer like his father had been.

But Henry Stokes, the headmaster of his school, had noticed that the boy was very brainy. He had seen Isaac designing and building a complicated system of sundials that worked as a very accurate clock. Stokes persuaded Isaac's mother to let him continue his studies. And in his final year in school, Isaac topped his class!

At Cambridge University, Isaac reverted to his old ways. He was not interested in cracking exams. Instead, he worked quietly in his room and developed what would one day be known as **calculus** – a branch of mathematics that deals with things that are constantly changing. Today, calculus is used in a huge number of areas, from medical research to computer science to making sure that the roof of your house does not fall on your head.

Richard Feynman, one of the greatest scientists of the twentieth century, said that calculus was the language God had used when creating the universe.

## Why Did the Apple Fall?

In 1665, while Newton was still a student at Cambridge, a terrible epidemic struck England. The university closed down and everyone was sent home. The entire country went into lockdown. It would be two years before life returned to normal, and in these two years of lockdown, Newton did some amazing work, all by himself, sitting in his cottage. For instance, he discovered gravity. He was only 23 years old.

What is gravity? A ball thrown upwards comes down because of the force of gravity. Gravity is the force that is responsible for what is called the 'large-scale structure' of the universe, a complex web of galaxies so vast that it is almost impossible to imagine. In fact, gravity is one of the ***four fundamental forces*** that make the universe what it is. The other three are the strong nuclear force, the weak nuclear force and the electromagnetic force. These forces hold the universe together. Without them, there would not be you and us, neither our earth nor stars and galaxies. We'll talk about the other three forces in Chapter 20.

The story goes that Newton discovered gravity when an apple fell on his head from a tree under which he was sitting in his mother's garden. No one knows whether this really happened. It most probably didn't, at least not in that exact manner. But Newton would have realized that there was some force present that caused things like apples to fall downwards and not rise upwards. He thought deeply about it and figured out that the force that causes an apple to fall is the same force that keeps the planets revolving around the sun.

Newton named this force 'gravity', from the Latin *gravitas*, meaning weight. He said that the force of gravity acts between any pair of objects. In the chapter on Copernicus, we briefly mentioned Johannes Kepler, who was a German mathematician and astronomer. Based on astronomical observations made by his mentor Tycho Brahe, Kepler formulated three laws about how planets move around the sun. It took a lot of math. Using the idea of gravity, Newton was able to derive these same laws.

The discovery of gravity had far-reaching consequences. By using the concept of gravity, two nineteenth-century astronomers John Couch Adams and Urbain Le Verrier were able to predict the existence of the planet Neptune before it was actually observed!

Adams (1819–1892), an English astronomer, and Le Verrier (1811–1877), a French mathematician, did not know each other, but both noticed that the way the planet Uranus, at that time the farthest planet known to Man, moved, did not seem to obey the laws that Kepler and Newton had proposed and proved. Both figured out that there had to be another planet beyond Uranus and its gravitational force caused the irregularities in Uranus' motion.

On 31 August 1846, Le Verrier sent a letter to the French Academy, saying that there is another planet and here is where it is. Two days later, Adams mailed his findings to the Royal Greenwich Observatory. On 23 September, the Berlin Observatory, based on La Verrier's calculations, sighted Neptune almost exactly where he had predicted it should be.

Adams seems to have been a true gentleman. When there was some dispute about which of them should get the credit for discovering Neptune, he wrote that 'there is no doubt that (Le Verrier's) researches were first published to the world, and led to the actual discovery of the planet . . ., so that the facts stated above cannot detract, in the slightest degree, from the credit due to M. Le Verrier.' As we will see later in the book, Newton was not such a gracious person.

## How Things Move

On 5 July 1687, Newton published his three-volume book, *Philosophiae Naturalis Principia Mathematica.* Today, physicists refer to it as simply the *Principia.* Perhaps **the most important book of physics** theory ever, it contains Newton's laws of motion, Newton's law of universal gravitation and a derivation of Kepler's laws of planetary motion. Physics, which was earlier a bunch of conjectures and hypotheses, could now be described using mathematics, especially calculus.

## The Fight over Calculus

The story of calculus is a bit complex. Some years after Newton had published his *Principia*, followed by several updated editions of the book, each of which carried longer explanations of his mathematical methods, the German mathematician and scientist Gottfried Wilhelm Leibniz accused him of stealing his work. Leibniz claimed that he had invented calculus. Newton denied that he had stolen anything, but a bitter fight began with Newton and other British scientists on one side and Leibniz and his supporters on the other. In fact, Newton's side said that it was Leibniz who had stolen from Newton. This war of words continued till Leibniz's death in 1716.

It is a fact that Leibniz published the first major paper on calculus in 1684, three years before Newton published his *Principia*. The word 'calculus' itself comes from the Latin title of that paper. Newton said he had begun working on a form of calculus in 1666, at the age of 23, but did not publish it. However, Newton did not reveal all the mysteries of his calculus till the third edition of *Principia*, which was published in 1704. By then, Leibniz had published several more papers on the subject.

Today, it is generally accepted that both men invented calculus, with neither knowing about the other's work. But mathematicians also agree that modern calculus owes more to the brilliant German than to the legendary Englishman. The calculus notation we commonly use, for example, is attributed to Leibniz.

Newton's laws are universal and can be used to explain any sort of motion in the macro world, the world we can see and feel – why things move the way they do. Whether one is sending rockets into space or playing a game of cricket or walking back home from school, the laws come into play.

What are these three laws?

The first is the **Law of Inertia**. It states: 'An object at rest stays at rest and an object in motion stays in motion with the same speed and in the same direction unless acted upon by an external unbalanced force.'

There's a football lying on an open field. It will keep lying there unless you decide to roll it, that is, apply an 'external unbalanced force'. And once you roll that ball, it will come to rest at some point. Here, 'external forces' – friction and wind – cause the ball to slow down and then stop moving. The ball rubs against the ground and there is resistance, which slows it down. If there is wind blowing against the direction in which the ball is moving, the ball will slow down faster. If there is no friction and no wind, which is not possible in the real world, the ball would keep moving forever, at the same speed in a straight line.

The second law is the **Law of Acceleration**. It says, 'The rate of change of momentum of an object is directly proportional to the force acting on the body and takes place in the same direction as the force.' This law quantifies motion. If you know the force acting on a body, you can determine the rate at which the body's speed – the physics term is actually 'velocity', which specifies both speed and direction – is changing.

This law explains why the harder you kick a football, the faster and farther it goes.

Both these laws were based on Galileo's work.

Newton's third law is the **Law of Action and Reaction**. 'To every action, there is an equal and opposite reaction.' This means that forces come in pairs. When two bodies interact, they exert equal and opposite forces on each other. If you push the wall with your hand, your hand will experience an equal force in the opposite direction. You will not feel that because the wall has far more weight – the physics term is 'mass' – than you have. But if you try banging your head against a wall, you will know. (Don't actually do this, of course!)

How do we walk? Our feet push the ground backwards and the ground pushes us forward. These two forces form an action and reaction pair. Action–reaction pairs are present everywhere throughout nature.

## Non-Contact Forces

The examples mentioned above are of contact forces – that is, when two bodies touch each other and exert force on each other. There are non-contact forces too, where objects do not touch each other.

Gravity, electrostatic and magnetic forces are all non-contact forces. The earth and the moon attract each other from a distance. Two magnets exert forces on each other from a distance. In each of these cases, we also have an action–reaction pair.

Newton also made significant contributions to the field of optics, that is, the study of light. People did not understand colour very well in those days. Strange as it may sound, philosophers were not sure whether colour resided in an object or in our minds. Newton showed that colour is a property of light, and that white light is a mixture of different colours.

Newton was one of the **most influential scientists ever**. His wide range of discoveries provided modern physics with a solid foundation. The most amazing thing is that his theories could be applied to the universe at large. His ideas were some of the first to explain the universe in a logical manner.

Part of the epitaph engraved on his tomb at Westminster Abbey in London reads: 'Mortals rejoice that there has existed such and so great an ornament of the human race!'

**Detective Newton**

Yes, Newton was also a detective! When he was made the head of the Royal Mint, which produced all the British coins, he estimated that 20 per cent of the coins being used by the public were fake. Gangs of counterfeiters were making serious profits, but the government was finding it very difficult to catch them or prove them guilty.

So, Newton got to work. Wearing disguises, he started visiting the taverns where criminals were thought to hang out and befriended some of them. He set up a band of informers, picked up clues and collected evidence.

He then made himself a 'Justice of the Peace' – a local magistrate with the power to deliver quick justice – and conducted the cases against the suspects. With Newton's efforts, 28 counterfeiters were convicted and England was rid of the menace of fake coins.

# 9

# The Men Who Gave Us Electricity

The human race survived some 200,000 years without electricity. But today, we cannot imagine going without this extremely useful form of energy for more than a few hours. The ease of life that electricity provides is the result of the work done by numerous physicists and inventors.

Electricity has always been around. Lightning is electricity, fish like the electric eel use electricity to kill other fish for food, and our brain uses electric signals to control everything we do. However, electricity was first understood, harnessed and put to use only between the seventeenth and nineteenth centuries.

## Static Electricity

If we comb our hair with a plastic comb, we can observe that the comb is able to attract small pieces of paper afterwards. How does this happen?

A comb is electrically neutral. It contains an equal number of positive and negative charges. But combing our hair causes a transfer of electrons from our hair to the comb and the comb gets negatively charged because electrons carry a negative charge. The charged comb induces an opposite charge in the paper and as opposite charges attract, the paper sticks to the comb. This is static electricity at work.

Thales of Miletus, whom we spoke about in Chapter 2, discovered static electricity when he found that amber – a fossil – could sometimes become 'animated' and attract dust particles. He described this phenomenon in the seventh century BCE.

## Positive and Negative

The first scientific treatment of electric phenomena was carried out in 1600 by William Gilbert, an English physician and physicist. He also studied magnetism and pointed out the difference between electricity and magnetism. He was the first person to say that the earth is a giant magnet. He gave the name 'electrics' to materials that exhibited properties similar to that of amber (the Greek word for amber is 'electron'). Diamond, sapphire, sulphur, resin and glass fell under this category. Metals and other materials, which were not electrifiable, he named 'non-electrics'. Gilbert also invented the electroscope, which is an instrument that can detect electrical charge.

The first electric generator was built by the German scientist Otto von Guericke in 1663. It produced static electricity with the help of friction. A ball of sulphur was rotated fast and when it was rubbed with a cloth, sparks flew. But for many years, no one could figure out if this was of any use. So generating static electricity this way just became a party game for rich Europeans.

Enter **Benjamin Franklin** (1706–1790). He was one of the smartest human beings of the eighteenth century. He was an author, political activist, publisher, scientist, diplomat and one of the Founding Fathers of the United States of America (USA). He was so multifaceted that many Americans today believe that he was once president of the US (even though he wasn't)! He did hold many important posts though. For instance, he was America's first ambassador to France and also governor of the state of Pennsylvania.

Franklin made significant contributions to the field of electricity. He was the first person to use the terms positive and negative charge. Through experiments, he discovered that when we rub two objects together, charge is not created. Rather, it is transferred from one object to the other. He also found that, in nature, all objects have an equal number of positive and negative charges. The principle of conservation of electricity is based on these two findings. Electrical charges never die. They just move.

Franklin created a basic electric battery using glass windowpanes and lead plates. He also experimented with Leyden jars, which were used to store and transfer charge in those days. The most well-known story associated with Franklin is his 'kite experiment', where he attached a long wire to a silken kite and used it to attract electric charges from storm clouds. By doing this, he was able to demonstrate the connection between lightning and electricity. The story, however, may not be fully true. We now know that he would possibly have been burnt to death by electrocution if he was actually holding the kite.

Franklin also discovered that when a pointed object is placed near a charged object, electricity gets transferred to the pointed object. He used this concept to invent the lightning rod, which is used even today to protect houses from a direct lightning strike. He also built a system of bells that sent warning signals when thunderclouds approached.

## Voltage, Current, Resistance

Luigi Galvani (1737–1790) was an Italian physician who lived in Bologna in the eighteenth century who discovered 'animal electricity' or 'bioelectricity'. He found that muscle and nerve cells produce electricity and observed that the muscles of dead frogs twitched when struck by an electric spark. Since then, many studies have found that electricity is produced in living organisms, including human beings, animals and plants. Chemical energy gets converted to electrical energy, which is then used by the body to govern the metabolism (chemical processes of life) and carry impulses along nerve fibres. Muscle contraction is also caused by an internal flow of electricity.

The **galvanometer**, the instrument that measures electrical current, is named after Galvani.

Alessandro Volta (1745–1827), who was a professor at Pavia in Italy, discovered that electricity could be generated by chemical means and made to flow through a conducting material in a closed circuit. He built the first battery known as a voltaic pile. It consisted of alternating copper and zinc discs. Each metal pair was separated by flannel soaked in a weak acid. The unit of electrical potential, the **volt**, is named after Alessandro Volta.

The next great contribution to electricity was made by Charles-Augustin de Coulomb (1736–1806). He gave us the mathematical equation that states that the force between two electrical charges is proportional to the product of the charges and inversely proportional to the square of the distance between them. This was the first time mathematics was applied to electricity. The unit of charge was named '**coulomb**' in his honour.

The next important physicist in this field was Georg Simon Ohm (1789–1854). He gave us **Ohm's Law**, which lays out the relationship between electrical current and voltage. Ohm's Law is very simple. It states that the current (I) flowing through a conductor is directly proportional to the voltage (V) across it and inversely proportional to the resistance (R).

$$I = V/R$$

You could think of the voltage as water pressure, the current as the amount of water flowing through a pipe and resistance as the width of the pipe. More water will flow through the pipe if there is greater pressure and also if the pipe is wider. Similarly, a larger current flows through a wire if the voltage is large and the resistance is low – low resistance being equivalent to a wider pipe.

Ohm's Law can be applied to metal conductors and electrical circuits. If two out of the three variables – voltage, current and resistance – are known, the third can be determined. However, the law cannot be applied to semiconductors and insulators. This is because semiconductors sometimes conduct electricity and sometimes not, while insulators never conduct electricity. Most modern electronics – the science of very small electrical currents – depend on semiconductors, such as our smartphones, digital cameras, washing machines, LED bulbs.

In time, based on the work of these men and others, scientists connected the two fields of electricity and magnetism. And electromagnetism came into being.

### Benjamin the Brilliant

Though Benjamin Franklin never became president of the US, he remains one of America's favourite heroes of all time. The $100 note carries his face.

Some fun facts about Franklin:

- Franklin was so popular as the American ambassador to France that his picture was used on jewellery, watches and snuffboxes. Fashionable ladies even got their hair styled to imitate the fur cap he wore.
- It was Franklin who wrote the line that parents the world over tell their children: 'Early to bed and early to rise makes a man healthy, wealthy and wise.'

- A keen chess player, he popularized the game in America. In 1999, he was inducted into the US Chess Hall of Fame.
- He invented a new version of the glass harmonica. His design was so innovative and unique that some of the greatest ever music composers, including Beethoven, Strauss and Mozart, created pieces especially for it.
- He wanted to fix English to make it more logical. He created a new alphabet, which got rid of six letters – C, J, W, Q, X and Y – that he thought were confusing, and added six new letters representing common sounds like 'ng,' 'sh' and 'th'. He hoped his system would improve spelling. Unfortunately, it never caught on.

# 10

# The Birth of Electromagnetism

In the last chapter, we spoke about the physicists who gave us electricity. Magnetism is another important branch of physics, and is closely related to electricity. Magnets play a critical role in our daily lives, though we may not be aware of this.

Computers have magnets built into them. They help store data in their hard drives. Magnets are also used in electrical generators, which convert mechanical energy to electricity. While recycling, we use electromagnets to separate metallic waste from non-metallic waste. Magnetic Resonance Imaging (MRI) machines employ magnets for their operation and are used to look inside your body. Most of the appliances we use at home – refrigerators, vacuum cleaners, telephones, doorbells and so on – have magnets in them.

Magnetism, like electricity, was discovered in ancient times, when people noticed that lodestones, which were naturally magnetized pieces of the mineral magnetite, could attract iron. Early scientists treated electricity and magnetism as separate fields.

## The Newton of Electricity

In 1820, Danish scientist Hans Christiaan Oersted discovered that electricity and magnetism were actually interrelated phenomena. He found that a magnetic needle was deflected when it was placed near a wire conducting electricity. This demonstrated that the conducting wire had magnetic properties. He shared this finding with the Academy of Sciences in Paris. French physicist Andre Marie Ampere was very excited by this finding and began to conduct his own research on the connection between the two fields.

Ampere found that two parallel wires conducting electricity could attract or repel each other depending on the direction of the flow of current. He gave us **Ampere's Law**, which describes the relation between the strength of the electric current and the magnetic field around it. Ampere also tried to understand the relationship between electricity and magnetism in physical terms and came up with the explanation that magnetism was caused by moving charged particles.

He theorized that permanent magnets were magnetic because of electric currents at the molecular level. 'Electrodynamic molecules' was the name he gave to moving charged particles. His hypothesis was correct. The particle is now known as the electron, and Ampere is regarded as the 'Newton of Electricity'.

Based on these discoveries, Ampere invented the solenoid and the first functional electric telegraph, which was then built up into the world's first long-distance electrical communication system by the American inventor Samuel Morse. A solenoid is a cylindrical coil of wire, which acts as a magnet when an electric current flows through it. It has many uses. For example, a doorbell. When you press a doorbell button, you complete an electrical circuit that allows electricity to flow through the doorbell's internal electromagnet. A solenoid in the circuit hits a bumper and the bell goes *ding-dong*.

For more than two centuries, before email and mobile phone texting were invented, the telegraph was the fastest way to send text messages over long distances. By switching solenoids on and off, the operator sent 'dots' and 'dashes' – electrical clicks – that translated into a message according to what was called the Morse Code. For instance, SOS – 'We are in danger and need help' – is three short taps, three long ones and three short ones again. For a very long time, the telegraph played a vital role in winning wars, striking business deals, maintaining law and order and even in the lives of common citizens who needed to get some news quickly to a loved one.

## The Father of Electricity

It is at this point in the story of physics that the great British scientist Michael Faraday (1791–1867) makes his appearance. He is sometimes referred to as the 'Father of Electricity'. He was born into a poor family and attended a local school till he was 13. Then, he worked as a trainee book binder to earn money to support his family.

Faraday's passion for science was kindled when he read a description of electricity in a copy of the *Encyclopaedia Britannica* that he was binding. He was so excited by what he read that he bought some apparatus and chemicals to check if what he was reading was true.

He kept reading and experimenting, and at the age of 19, went to watch the great chemist Sir Humphry

Davy speak at the prestigious Royal Institute and Royal Society. Sir Humphry was an amazing scientist. He invented the Davy Safety Lamp, which reduced the risk of miners deep under the earth getting killed due to explosions caused by methane and other gases that catch fire easily. If there were gases around that could cause a fire, the flame in the lamp burned higher, warning the miner. And if there was too little oxygen deep down the mine for the miner to breathe easily, the flame would go out. The Davy lamp may have saved thousands of lives.

Using electricity, Davy isolated (and therefore discovered) several elements, including potassium, sodium, calcium, barium and magnesium. During his experiments with nitrous oxide, Davy was astonished at how it made him laugh. So he nicknamed it **'laughing gas'** and wrote that it could be used to relieve pain during surgery. Two and a quarter centuries after Davy's discovery, even after more sophisticated anaesthetics have been synthesized, laughing gas is still commonly used to start off the process, before the patient is given a more powerful anaesthetic.

Racing cars use nitrous oxide to release more oxygen inside the engine, releasing and burning more fuel, which gives the car more power. And this versatile gas is also used to make delicious whipped cream!

After listening to Davy speak, Faraday, only 20 years old at the time, sent him a 300-page book of notes that he had taken during these lectures. Davy was very impressed. So when he damaged his eyes – in fact, he went blind for a few days – in an experiment-related accident, he appointed Faraday as a chemical assistant at the Royal Institute.

The two appear to have continued Davy's legacy of conducting dangerous experiments that blew things up, because soon after starting to work together, both of them were seriously injured in a test involving nitrogen trichloride – a nasty liquid that has to be handled very carefully.

But while he was surviving the regular explosions in Davy's laboratory, Faraday was also doing his own stuff. He found that he could obtain an electric current in a conductor by varying the magnetic fields around it. This effect is known as **electromagnetic induction**. Electromagnetic induction has many uses. Generators, which produce electricity use this principle. So do transformers that transfer electrical energy from one circuit to another. The discovery of electromagnetic induction was a milestone not only for science but for society as a whole. Suddenly, it was possible to generate electricity on a large scale in power stations and transfer it. So, people's lives underwent a dramatic change.

Faraday was also the first person to introduce the concept of fields and lines of force. These were important concepts, which helped in the understanding of electrical and magnetic phenomena and the further development of physics. Our understanding of fields plays a great role in quantum theory, an area of physics that Faraday could not have imagined.

*In 1831, Michael Faraday demonstrated the Faraday wheel, a simple electrical generator. As the wheel turns, electrons flow to the rim from the centre (or from the rim to centre depending on direction of rotation), which generates a current.*

## Maxwell's Equations

The person who unified electricity and magnetism and gave a mathematical foundation to the field of electromagnetism was nineteenth-century Scottish mathematician and physicist James Clerk Maxwell (1831–1879). He gave us four elegant equations that describe all electrical and magnetic phenomena. Unfortunately, he used such high-level mathematics to derive these equations that it took the physicists of that era a long time to fully figure out the workings and accept the implications.

When taken together, Maxwell's equations predict the existence of **electromagnetic waves**. An electromagnetic wave is a wave that travels at the speed of light and is made up of oscillating electric and magnetic fields. Light, radio waves, X-rays and microwaves are all electromagnetic waves.

Today, we depend a lot on electromagnetic waves to run our technologies and our lives. From satellites up in the skies and the microwave ovens in our kitchens to the cell phones we use and the most advanced astronomical telescopes, all run on electromagnetic waves.

Since Maxwell united the three different fields – electricity, magnetism and light – so beautifully, he is regarded by some as the third-greatest physicist ever. We are sure you can guess who the other two are. We have talked about one of them already, and the other will appear later in the book.

Maxwell also contributed to various other areas of science – geometrical optics, thermodynamics, bridge structures, and so on. He observed that Saturn's ring must be composed of small particles, not rocks. He also investigated colour vision and concluded that almost all the colours we see are combinations of three primary colours – red, green and blue. Even today, after many later discoveries and variations, the RGB (red-green-blue) colour model is used in many electronic devices, including cameras, and television and computer screens.

Based on his colour model, Maxwell was able to produce the first-ever colour photograph. Today, it looks far from perfect, because the lenses and filters of that time were primitive. But with this practical demonstration, Maxwell proved that his colour theory was the right way forward.

# 11

# The Story of Light

Light is a fundamental component of our lives and the way the universe works. But what is light? Today we know that light is an electromagnetic wave. The visible part of light is a small part of that electromagnetic spectrum, with other parts being infrared rays, X-rays, gamma rays, microwaves, radio waves and ultraviolet rays.

How do we see things? What are the properties of light? How does light interact with matter? What instruments can we use to detect light? How do we see colour? How can we put light to use? The branch of physics known as optics developed as a result of scientists asking these questions.

In ancient times, people were awed by light and

thought it was of supernatural origin. Ancient Egyptians believed that the light of day emanated from the eyes of Ra, the sun god. The Bible also treats light as divine. The Book of Genesis, the first book of the Old Testament, gives an account of Creation in which God created light before creating the stars and planets.

And because of the divine nature attributed to it, light is said to be good while the dark is considered evil. Of course, scientists do not believe this. As we will see later, about 95 per cent of our universe is 'dark', consisting of matter and energy that we cannot see!

## The Way We See

The Greek philosophers were the first people who tried to explain the nature of light. Today, we know how the process of vision takes place. Light reflected by objects enters our eyes through the pupil, a black hole in the centre of the iris. Depending on the amount of light present, the iris changes the size of the pupil to let in the optimum amount of light. The light rays pass through a crystalline lens in our eyes and an upside-down image of the object is formed on the back surface of the eyes, known as the retina. The retina then sends electrical signals to our brain. This is how the brain is able to perceive the object.

All this knowledge was not available to the ancient Greeks. Most of them believed that the eyes emitted light, which fell on objects and illuminated them. They were not able to explain vision in a satisfactory manner because they did not have the means to study the eye. Moreover, they thought they could explain everything using a sense of geometry.

## Eyes and Rays

Euclid, the Greek mathematician who lived around 300 BCE, put forth a number of properties of light that turned out to be accurate. He said that light travels in straight lines, and when it undergoes reflection, the angle of incidence equals the angle of reflection. That is, if light falls on a surface at an angle of 45 degrees, it will bounce off in the other direction at a 45-degree angle.

The process of vision was correctly explained by the Arab scientist Al-Hazen in the eleventh century CE. He noticed that we feel pain when we gaze directly at a bright object and continue to see after-images for a while. From these observations, he concluded that light travels from the object to the eye, not the other way around. He performed dissections on the eye and was able to describe its anatomy. Not all the conclusions he drew from this were correct, but his work was very valuable to later scientists.

## The Birth of Spectacles

Towards the end of the thirteenth century, Italian glassworkers found that they could correct vision with the help of lenses. But no one knew why this was so and the general belief was that lenses had some magical properties.

It was much later, in 1604, that Johannes Kepler studied the transmission of light rays through lenses using geometric optics. He used the results to study image formation in the eye and concluded that vision was caused by the formation of inverted images at the retina. He was also able to explain how lenses could correct vision.

Towards the end of the sixteenth century, Dutch spectacle-makers combined two lenses and were able to see magnified images of distant objects. This was the birth of the telescope. Kepler gave a theoretical explanation of the workings of lenses and the telescope. Galileo realized the scientific significance of this and built his own telescopes. Using this, he was able to observe the moons of Jupiter. This provided clinching evidence that Copernicus's Heliocentric Theory was correct, but as we have seen, it also got Galileo into a lot of trouble.

## The Particles of Light

Over the years, there have been many attempts to explain the nature of light. The **Corpuscular Theory of Light** was one such attempt. The ancient Greek philosopher Democritus contended that all matter is composed of tiny indivisible particles. This idea was carried over to light by the French scientist and philosopher Rene Descartes. Newton formalized the theory.

According to this theory, light consists of tiny particles of matter known as 'corpuscles'. These particles are emitted by sources of light, and they travel in straight lines with different velocities in different media. Lights of different colours consist of different sizes of particles. Vision is produced when these particles land upon the retina of the eye.

Reflection can be explained very well using this theory because light is reflected in exactly the same way a ball bounces when it hits a surface. When a ball hits a surface perpendicularly, which is a 90 degree angle, it bounces back along the same path – just like light does.

When it hits the surface at a different angle, it follows the same path a reflected beam of light would take.

Newton also explained the refraction of light – the way it bends when it passes through, say, glass – by assuming that the speed of light is greater in denser media. However, it has since been found that light actually travels more slowly in denser media. Newton's Corpuscular Theory was also unable to explain certain other phenomena related to light.

## That Wavy Thing

Some scientists observed that when an object was placed directly in front of a source of light, some light still passed around it. This meant that light was actually bending around the object. If it was made of tiny particles and moved only in a straight line, this would not have been possible. This phenomenon was named **diffraction**. The wave theory of light proposed by the English polymath Robert Hooke and the Dutch physicist Christiaan Huygens was better able to explain diffraction.

According to this theory, light has a wave-like nature. It travels as small spherical waves that add up to form a 'wavefront'. The wavefront produces new, secondary waves. This process repeats itself over and over again, resulting in the propagation of light. In addition to diffraction, reflection and refraction of light could be explained very satisfactorily using this model. The wave theory also predicted that the speed of light is less in denser media.

All of us have seen the colours of the rainbow appearing inside soap bubbles. This is a phenomenon called interference of light. It can be explained only if we assume that light consists of waves. If you have two waves originating from two different sources meeting up, they 'interfere' with each other when their paths cross. The wall of the soap bubble is extremely thin, so both sides of the wall reflect the light that falls on it. The two reflections, each with its seven visible colours, overlap and produce this rainbow-like effect. When one reflected wave meets the other at its peak, they push each other up and become visible. Similarly, if the two waves meet when they are at their bottom, they drag each other down and become invisible.

In 1801, British scientist Thomas Young performed the **'double-slit experiment'**. Similar experiments would be performed many times in the next two centuries to understand the nature of light. Young made light from a single source – a sharp beam – pass through two vertical slits on a metal plate to land on a screen behind it. The light waves passing through the slits interfered with each other, producing bright and dark bands on the screen. This showed that light was a wave, not made of particles.

Or that is what Young thought.

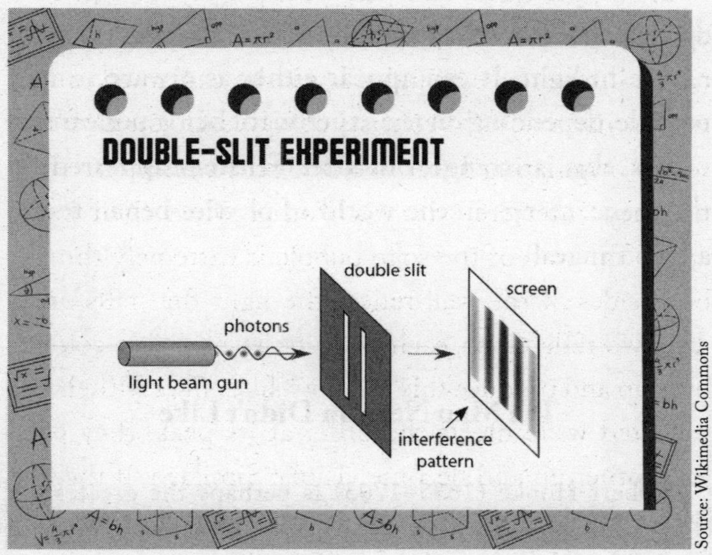


Source: Wikimedia Commons

In the early twentieth century, Albert Einstein, then a clerk in a government office in Berne, Switzerland, boldly stated that light consists of tiny packets of energy. He was able to explain the photoelectric effect with the help of this assumption. We will get into the details of the photoelectric effect in Chapter 17, but Einstein came to this conclusion because he observed that when light interacts with matter, it behaves as though it consists of tiny particles, each carrying a lump of energy. These tiny particles are now called photons.

Does this mean that the wave theory of light was discarded? No. Modern physicists attribute a dual nature to light. It can appear either as a wave or as a particle, depending on the experiment being performed.

Yes, this is strange, but after Einstein appeared on the scene, things in the world of physics began to get a lot stranger!

**The Man Newton Didn't Like**

Robert Hooke (1635–1703) is perhaps the greatest scientist that you have never heard of. He made huge contributions in an amazing range of fields and much of our world is built on what he discovered and proved. The mistake he made was to challenge Newton. Newton was much cleverer in a practical sense and far more powerful than him. As a result, he managed to get Hooke more or less wiped out of the history of science. Hooke's genius was fully recognized only 300 years later!

It was Hooke who discovered what 'air' is – that it is made up of particles, that it can be expanded or compressed, and what its relationship is to how we breathe. He designed the finest microscope of his time and proved that the world of the very small is as rich and complex as the one that we see around us. He invented the word 'cell' for all those tiny things that make up our bodies and other stuff.

His work on how materials respond to stress and strain has become fundamental to how we build things today, from dolls to malls. His discoveries have been used to make accurate watches for centuries. He was also the first person to suggest what would become Charles Darwin's theory of evolution 200 years later.

As an astronomer, Hooke found that the planet Jupiter rotates, described the centre of gravity of the earth and the moon, proposed that the earth's orbit around the sun is not a circle but an ellipse, and worked out the laws of how the planets move *before* Newton. He also developed the wave theory of light, which showed that Newton's theory of light might not be correct.

As an architect, he designed some great buildings like the Royal Greenwich Observatory – the 'zero point' from which the world gets its times, and the Royal College of Physicians in London. His idea that roads in cities should be placed in a grid pattern has been used by city planners across the world, from Washington DC to Chandigarh.

When Newton published his great work *Principia Mathematica*, Hooke protested that much of the stuff, including the laws of gravity that Newton was claiming to have discovered, were basically his and that he had told Newton about them much before *Principia* was written. Newton hit back and won. No one listened to Hooke.

It took Hooke 300 years to get his due, and today, he is referred to as the 'British Leonardo da Vinci'.

# 12

# The Building Blocks of Matter

How do we define matter? Matter is something that has mass and takes up space. The universe is made up of matter. Pondering over the wide variety of matter present in the universe can be quite mind-boggling. However, all these different kinds of matter are made up of the same building blocks, or atoms.

As we saw in the previous chapters, the idea of the atom had been thought up by philosophers both in ancient India and ancient Greece. But it was only in 1803 that British scientist Sir John Dalton gave us the modern and scientific definition of the atom. By the early twentieth century, people finally understood the structure of the atom.

The word 'atom' is derived from 'atomos', which is what Democritus called these tiny pieces of matter. It means indivisible. Democritus believed that atoms of different substances varied in size and shape, were in constant motion inside a void, and constantly collided with each other. During these collisions, they could stick together or fly apart. He proposed that changes taking place in matter resulted from dissociations or combinations of the atoms as they moved through the void.

Aristotle rejected this notion, and as we have seen before, everyone usually accepted whatever Aristotle said as the truth. So, the theory remained unexplored for 2,000 years.

## Dalton's Basics

In 1803, Dalton made a bold attempt to describe matter in terms of atoms and their properties. This is what we know as Dalton's Atomic Theory. He stated that all matter is made up of indivisible particles known as atoms. Atoms of a given element have identical mass and properties. According to this theory, compounds are a combination of two or more different kinds of atoms, and during a chemical reaction, a rearrangement of atoms takes place. Dalton was mostly correct, except for two things: an atom consists of even smaller particles (sub-atomic particles) and two atoms of the same element *can* have different masses.

Dalton's theory was based on two laws that had been discovered earlier. The first is the **Law of Conservation of Mass**, which states that matter can be neither created nor destroyed in a closed system. A closed system is, for example, a box or a room with such strong walls that nothing, not a breath of matter, air or energy, can enter from outside. We believe our universe, too, to be a closed system (just a very large one). This means that whenever we have a chemical reaction, the amount of each element present must be the same before and after the reaction. This is why we balance chemical equations.

The second law, which forms the basis of Dalton's Atomic Theory, is the **Law of Constant Composition**. This law states that a pure compound will always have the same proportion of the same elements. For example, carbon dioxide, which is made up of one carbon and two oxygen atoms, contains the same proportion of carbon and oxygen no matter where and how the gas is produced. These two laws led Dalton to believe that matter consisted of tiny particles that could neither be created nor destroyed and that when atoms combine to form molecules, they do so in specific proportions.

Dalton's atomic theory was a good start in our journey of understanding the nature of matter. But at this point, not much was known about atoms themselves, and for a while, there was little progress in this area of physics.

### Weather, Colours, Chemistry

John Dalton (1766–1844) is most widely known for his Atomic Theory, but he did a lot of other stuff too.

He seems to have been a child prodigy. When he was only 12 years old, his older brother, Jonathan, took over the school that John was studying in and made him a teacher! Two years later, the brothers purchased another school where they taught around 60 students.

At the age of 27, Dalton published his first book, *Meteorological Observations and Essays*. No one paid much attention at that time, but we now know that the book practically invented meteorology – the study of weather. Till then, people in the West had been explaining weather through general folklore and myths.

A year or so later, he published a paper describing the defect he had discovered in his own and his brother's vision. This paper was the first known examination of colour blindness, which for many years after that was known as Daltonism!

It took years for Dalton's Atomic Theory to receive widespread recognition, but once it did, Dalton was amply rewarded. He was elected to the Royal Society, which, at that time, comprised the world's greatest scientists. The French Academy of Sciences made him one of its only eight foreign associates. He also received a pension from the British Crown. When he passed away, he was given the equivalent of a state funeral by the people of Manchester, where he had spent the last 50 years of his life. He was one of the city's most famous men of his time. He was also, despite his wealth, the city's most famous miser!

## Inside the Atom

In the late 1800s, the English physicist J.J. Thomson discovered the presence of negatively charged particles within an atom. When an airless glass tube was fitted with two electrodes – the positively charged anode and the negatively charged cathode – and a voltage was applied across the tube, certain rays were observed emanating from the cathode. These were named cathode rays.

Thomson experimented with cathode rays and found that these rays consisted of negatively charged particles. By taking measurements, he found that these particles had a mass that was 1/2,000th of a hydrogen atom. The same rays were obtained after changing the metal the cathode was made of. So, he concluded that these negatively charged particles were present in all types of matter and that the atom was not the final building block. There were things inside it.

Thomson's model of the atom is now known as the **Plum Pudding Model**. Plum pudding is an English dessert. In Thomson's model, the atom was seen as a ball of jelly-like material (pudding) with a positive charge, and the electrons were stuck in it like plums. But this theory did not last long. It was soon disproved by one of Thomson's students, Ernest Rutherford.

Rutherford was a physicist from New Zealand who studied at Cambridge University under the guidance of Thomson. He received the Nobel Prize in 1908 for his research work on the chemistry of radioactive substances. A few years later, he thought up an experiment that would tell us more about the structure of atoms. He wanted to confirm Thomson's model, but to his surprise, the experiment proved exactly the opposite.

During the experiment, positively charged particles, known as alpha particles, were fired at a thin sheet of gold foil. Alpha particles are really tiny and can pass very easily through gold foil. Thomson's understanding was that the positive charge would be spread over the entire atom and the alpha particles should pass through with little or no deflection.

Most of the particles behaved as he expected and passed through the foil with very little deflection. However, a small number of particles were deflected through very large angles from their original paths. This was completely unexpected. The only way these results could be explained was by assuming that the positive charge is not spread all over the atom but is concentrated in a small dense core at the centre of the atom. And the rest of the atom is empty. Rutherford now proposed a new model of the atom, in which electrons orbit a tiny positively charged core, which he called 'nucleus'. It is from 'nucleus' that the term 'nuclear physics' was born.

We owe the discovery of the proton also to Rutherford. In 1917, he performed the first artificially induced nuclear reaction by carrying out experiments in which nitrogen nuclei were bombarded with alpha particles. As a result, he discovered the emission of a positively charged sub-atomic particle, which he initially called the 'hydrogen atom'. Later he named it a 'proton' and that is the name that we universally use today.

Rutherford didn't stop there. He went on to develop the atomic numbering system, which forms one of the foundations of modern chemistry.

## The Birth of Quantum Physics

This is the point where a Danish physicist named Niels Bohr enters our story, and physics takes a whole new turn. Bohr realized that classical physics could not fully explain what was going on at the sub-atomic level. He guessed that using quantum theory could be the right way to go about it.

Quantum mechanics is a branch of physics that tries to explain what happens at the sub-atomic level. It was developed around the mid-1920s by Bohr, Erwin Schrodinger, Werner Heisenberg, Max Born and other great scientists, to explain observations that did not make sense according to the laws of classical physics.

In **Bohr's model of the atom**, we have a small, dense, positively charged nucleus with electrons orbiting around it in fixed paths, somewhat like the solar system where the planets go around the sun. This model is the one most people are familiar with. It explains many phenomena such as chemical bonding – when atoms get together to form molecules – and why electrons don't get absorbed into the nucleus. However, the model had some drawbacks. While it explained the hydrogen atom well, it could not explain observations for heavier elements.

In 1926, the Austrian physicist Erwin Schrodinger proposed that electrons don't move in fixed orbits or shells, but behave like waves instead. This may sound a bit odd, but remember that light can behave both as a particle and as a wave. It turned out that electrons, too, have a dual nature.

Schrodinger gave us an equation to help us determine the position of electrons. This equation does not tell us where an electron is at a particular instance but gives us the *probability* of finding electrons at a particular place – that there's, say, an 80 per cent chance that it's *here*.

In 1932, English physicist James Chadwick, under Rutherford's guidance, completed the picture of our atom by discovering the neutron. So we now had a model of an atom with a dense nucleus at the centre consisting of neutrons and protons, and electrons orbiting this nucleus in a cloud around it.

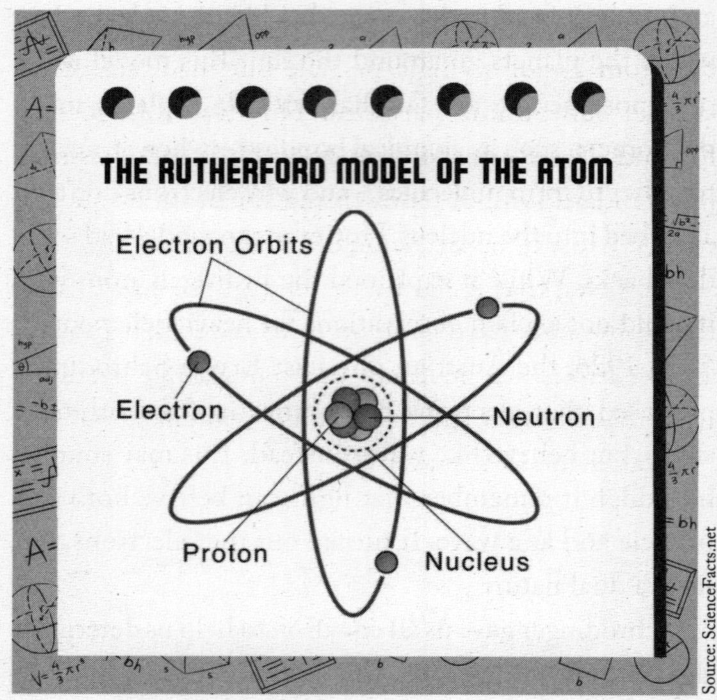


Source: ScienceFacts.net

With this discovery, Rutherford could explain the atomic number of a chemical element, which defines that element. For an ordinary nucleus composed of protons and neutrons, this is equal to the number of protons. This is because neutrons carry no charge. In an ordinary atom that carries no charge, the atomic number is also equal to the number of electrons – the positive and negative charges cancel out.

Rutherford's discovery led scientists to realize that the atom is not a single particle but made up of far smaller sub-atomic particles. This was a huge step forward. The 'Rutherford model', as it is called, is now the standard symbol representing the atom or nuclear energy. Most of us are familiar with it.

However, that is hardly the end of the story. Since then, physicists have gone on to discover that protons and neutrons are made up of even smaller particles, which they have named quarks. We will talk about this in more detail in Chapter 20.

**Why Quark?**

In 1964, American physicist Murray Gell-Mann proposed that protons and neutrons were made up of smaller particles. So what would these particles be called? Gell-Mann had a habit of using names like 'squeak' and 'squork' for peculiar objects, so he decided to name his discovery 'quork'.

Some months later, he came across a line in Irish writer James Joyce's novel *Finnegans Wake*: 'Three quarks for Muster Mark!'

*Finnegans Wake* is possibly the most difficult-to-read novel ever written in English. Very few people have managed to finish it and even fewer people have understood what it is all about. But Gell-Mann thought 'quark' was a nice name for these particles, because according to his calculations, they came in bunches of threes.

So 'quark' it was. We now know that there are six types of quarks, and they are named up, down, strange, charm, top and bottom. In Chapter 20, we'll look at quarks more closely.

# 13

# Heat as Energy

We need heat and warmth to stay alive. But what is heat? We can touch something and make out whether an object is hot or cold. But our sense of touch is not very reliable. Try placing your left hand in hot water and your right hand in cold water, then put both your hands in water at room temperature. Your left hand will feel as though the water is cold, while your right hand will tell you that the same water is warm.

Today we know that heat is a form of energy that an object possesses because of the motion of atoms and molecules moving inside it. The faster these particles move, the hotter is the object. Cold objects also possess energy. It is just that their atoms and molecules are moving at a much slower pace. Heat is transferred between two systems or bodies having different temperatures. It flows from a higher temperature to a lower temperature.

Fire was the first source of heat that ancient people learnt to control and use – for warmth and lighting, protection from wild animals, creating advanced hunting tools and cooking food. So it makes sense that the ancients believed that heat was a property of fire.

## How Hot Is It Really?

Heat could be studied scientifically only when the thermometer came into existence. The first known thermometer was the **Galileo thermometer**, invented in 1596. Even though it was called Galileo thermometer, he was not the one who made it. It was invented by a group of scholars and technicians in Florence, Italy, who based their device on ideas that Galileo had expressed nearly 60 years before.

Galileo had discovered the principles on which the thermometer was built: buoyancy and the variation in density based on temperature. The Galileo thermometer consists of a sealed glass tube filled with a clear liquid and small bulbs partly filled with coloured liquids floating inside it. When there is a change in temperature, the bulbs rise or sink to different levels. The temperature is determined by finding out which bulb sinks the most.

Strictly speaking, the Galileo thermometer is not a thermometer but a thermoscope. The difference between the two is that while a thermometer gives us the exact temperature, a thermoscope gives us the difference in temperatures. In 1612, the Italian inventor Santorio Santorio – yes, that was his name – added a numerical scale to his thermoscope and created the first crude version of a clinical thermometer. It could be placed in a patient's mouth to find out their body temperature. However, neither of these two thermometers was very accurate.

The first person to use mercury in the thermometer – which is what modern thermometers use – was German-Polish scientist Daniel Gabriel Fahrenheit (1686–1736). The expansion of liquid mercury is very predictable and with improved glass-working techniques, this thermometer was much more precise.

## Men Who Became Units 1: Fahrenheit

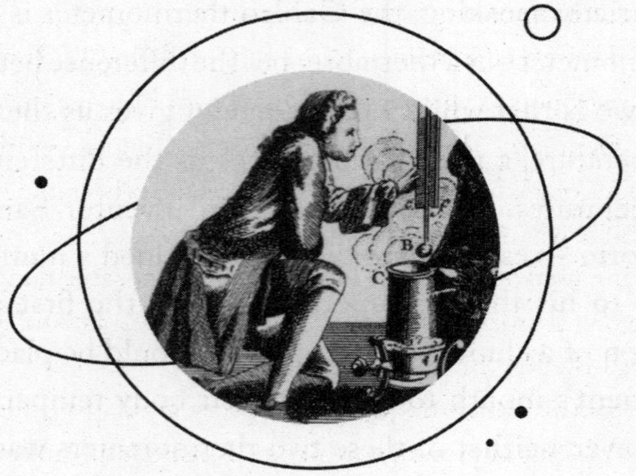


Source: Wikimedia Commons

*Daniel Gabriel Fahrenheit*

Daniel Gabriel Fahrenheit (1686–1736) was a German-Polish scientist who invented the first truly accurate thermometer. Countries such as the US use the Fahrenheit scale to measure all temperatures, from forest fires to how warm a hamburger is. In India, we use it only for body temperature.

Fahrenheit was only 16 years old when his parents passed away. Even though he was deeply interested in science, his new guardians forced him to take a four-year accounting course in Amsterdam. He went through with it, but once it was over, he ran away from Holland. His guardians were very angry and went to the Dutch police, and a warrant was issued for his arrest.

However, Fahrenheit found support from Ole Romer, an astronomer who was then the mayor of Copenhagen in Denmark. The arrest warrant was dropped. Within a few years, he had invented his mercury thermometer, which was much better than the alcohol-based ones being used at that time. His device soon became famous among European scientists. He returned to Poland and began selling his thermometers.

But it seems that he was not very good at business. He ran out of money, returned to Amsterdam and spent the last year of his life living in a friend's home. When he passed away, he was given a 'fourth-class funeral', which was for people with no money or home. He was only 50 years old.

Fahrenheit and Celsius are the two temperature scales that we use. Some countries like the US use the Fahrenheit scale, while others like India use the Celsius (or centigrade) scale. However, all thermometers that we use to check our body temperature are graded on the Fahrenheit scale. When we say that a person is running a fever of 102 degrees, their body temperature is 102 degrees Fahrenheit.

## Men Who Became Units 2: Celsius

Source: Wikimedia Commons

*Anders Celsius*

In India and most other countries, we use the Celsius scale to measure temperature, except when we are using a thermometer to check for fever. Anders Celsius (1701–1744) was born 16 years after Fahrenheit, in Sweden, to a family of several astronomers and mathematicians.

He took to astronomy and published many pioneering works. He was the first to suggest a connection between the auroras borealis and australis– the brilliant displays of lights that occur in the skies from autumn to spring near the Arctic and Antarctic circles – and the magnetic field of the earth. He went on expeditions and made measurements that proved Newton's idea that our planet is not a perfect sphere but mostly spherical and flat at the two poles.

In 1742, Celsius proposed his temperature scale with a thermometer that had a scale of 0 degrees for the boiling point of water and 100 for the freezing point.

Celsius died of tuberculosis when he was only 43. A year after his death, his scale was reversed by the great Swedish biologist Carl Linnaeus, to make it more practical. So we now have 0 as freezing point and 100 when water boils.

## Gas Matters

The barometer – an instrument used to measure the pressure of gases – was invented in 1644. Using the barometer and an accurate thermometer, scientists were able to conduct experiments on gases to determine the relationship between temperature, pressure and volume of a fixed mass of gas. This enabled them to study heat scientifically, and the four famous gas laws came into being.

In 1662, the British scientist Robert Boyle studied the relationship between the volume and pressure of a fixed amount of gas at constant temperature and concluded that the volume of the gas is inversely proportional to its pressure. This means that if you reduce the volume of a given mass of gas to half of its original volume by squeezing it into a smaller space, without changing the temperature, its pressure is doubled. This is known as **Boyle's Law.**

**Charles' Law**, named after the French scientist Jacques Charles, gives us a way to calculate the change in the volume of a gas when it is heated. It states that when the pressure of a gas is constant, its temperature and volume are directly proportional to each other. That is, if the temperature drops, the volume will shrink; if the temperature rises, the volume will increase. This law seems to suggest that the volume of a gas will vanish at a certain temperature, what scientists call 'Absolute Zero'.

About half a century after Charles published his findings, the British polymath Lord Kelvin proved that Absolute Zero is roughly -273.15 Celsius or -459.67 Fahrenheit. However, all real gases change in form to solid or liquid at temperatures above Absolute Zero, so the question of vanishing does not arise. What actually happens is that the energy of gas molecules is minimal near Absolute Zero.

## Men Who Became Units 3: Kelvin

*Lord Kelvin*

While we talk of temperature in Celsius or Fahrenheit, scientists measure it in 'kelvins'. This unit is named after Lord Kelvin (1824–1907), who figured out the correct value of Absolute Zero, the ultimate lowest temperature: around −273.15 degrees Celsius or −459.67 degrees Fahrenheit. Lord Kelvin's work ranged from mathematics and physics (light, heat, electricity) to geology (working out the age of our planet) to engineering (laying thousands of miles of cables under the sea that carried telegraph messages between Europe and America).

Born as William Thomson, he was the first scientist to be made a lord. For some years, he did not agree with Joule's theory that mechanical work produced the same amount of heat energy as the energy spent in doing the work. But then he came to agree with Joule and worked with him to take the theory forward.

Late in his life, he wrote: 'When you can measure what you are speaking about and express it in numbers you know something about it; but when you cannot measure it, when you cannot express it in numbers, your knowledge is of a meagre and unsatisfactory kind: it may be the beginning of knowledge, but you have scarcely, in your thoughts, advanced to the stage of *science*, whatever the matter may be.'

In 1873, three years after his wife had died, Lord Kelvin became friends with the Blandy family who lived in Madeira in Portugal. A year later, then 70 years old, he sailed to Madeira again. As his ship neared the harbour, he signalled through the undersea cables he had laid to Frances Anna Blandy: 'Will you marry me?' Fanny signalled back. 'Yes'. They got married a month later.

**Gay-Lussac's Law,** named after French chemist Joseph Louis Gay-Lussac, gives us a relation between the pressure exerted by a gas on the walls of its container and the absolute temperature when the volume is kept constant. He found the pressure to be directly proportional to the temperature. If the temperature rises, the pressure rises.

The fourth is **Avogadro's Law,** named after Italian physicist Amedeo Avogadro. This law states that under the same conditions of temperature and pressure, equal volumes of gases contain an equal number of molecules.

Each of the four gas laws is based on the 'ideal' behaviour of gases. However, they become less accurate at very high temperatures and pressures. When you combine these four laws, you get the Combined Gas Law, which is critical when it comes to predicting the weather or understanding the climate.

## Lavoisier's Calories

In 1789, the French scientist Antoine Lavoisier proposed the first reasonable scientific explanation of heat. He pictured heat as an invisible, tasteless, odourless, weightless substance, which he called the **caloric fluid.** He postulated that hot bodies contain more of this fluid than cold bodies. He also suggested that the particles of the caloric fluid repel each other, causing heat to flow from hot bodies to cold bodies, when two bodies are kept in contact. According to Lavoisier, bodies could hold only a certain amount of the caloric fluid.

He derived the word 'caloric' from the Latin 'calor', which meant 'heat'.

Lavoisier's theory was proved wrong soon after, but the term 'calorie' lives on. A calorie is a unit of measurement, like a metre or a kilogram. Calories are the amount of energy released when your body digests and absorbs food. The more calories a food has, the more energy it can provide to your body.

Benjamin Thompson, also known as Count von Rumford, made a remarkable discovery in 1797. He found that heat was generated during the process of boring of cannons, in which drills and other metal instruments are used to hollow out the cannon barrel. The metal turned red-hot. He held a public demonstration where he bored a cannon with the barrel placed in a tank of cold water. After two and a half hours, the water was boiling even though he had not used any fire. The friction between the metals during the boring process was enough. This amazed scientists at that time.

Thompson's finding – that the internal energy of a system can be changed by doing work on the system, without adding any heat to it from outside – challenged the caloric fluid idea. How could friction produce an unlimited amount of heat? After all, if heat were a fluid, it would run out at some point and the metals would cool down on their own.

Scientists were now able to form a logical connection between heat and motion. They discarded the earlier concept of heat as a fluid and concluded that it is the motion of the molecules of a substance that gives rise to heat energy. They also concluded that the temperature of a body is an indication of the internal energy present in it.

The English scientist William Prescott Joule was inspired to take exact measurements and find out the 'mechanical equivalent of heat' – how much work needs to be done in order to produce one unit of heat.

## The Three Laws of the Universe

The first commercially viable steam engine was invented by the Scottish engineer James Watt in 1776. Scientists could now study heat in much more detail. From their observations, a new branch of physics known as thermodynamics was born. Thermodynamics studies relations between heat and other forms of energy. There are three laws of thermodynamics, which can be applied

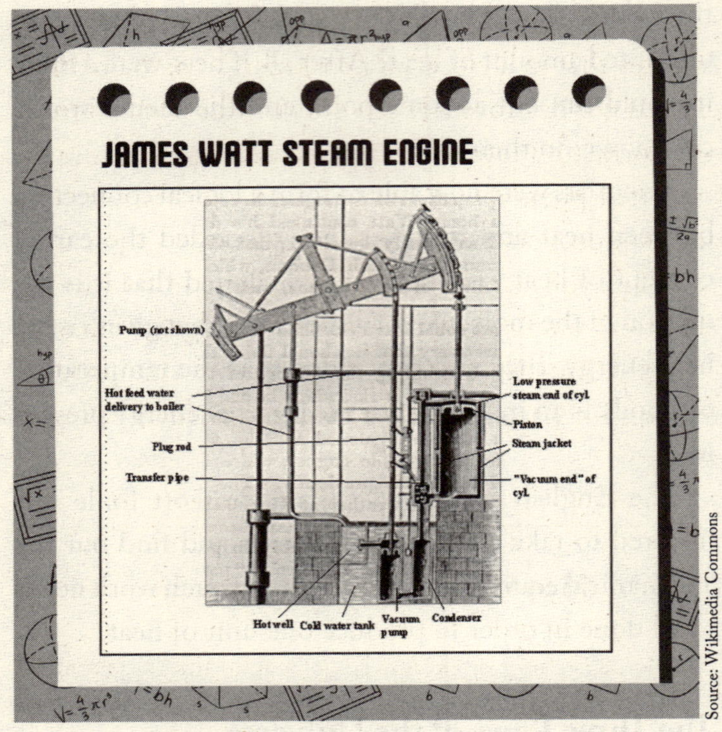


Source: Wikimedia Commons

*James Watt's steam engine directly powered the Industrial Revolution in Britain and changed the course of human history. The steam engine was a key factor in building the British Empire.*

to any system – from a microwave oven to the universe at large.

These laws are three of the most fundamental principles that govern the universe.

The first law is the **Law of Conservation of Energy**. It states that in a closed system, energy can be neither created nor destroyed. It can only be transformed from one form to another. This explained how seemingly unrelated phenomena, such as heat and light or heat and motion, could actually be related.

When you switch on an electric lamp in your room, electrical energy gets converted to light and heat energies, but the amount of energy in the universe remains unchanged. Only a tiny bit of it has changed its form.

### Men Who Became Units 4: Joule

A joule is a unit of energy. To go back to the apple that supposedly fell on Newton's head when he sat under a tree, a joule is the amount of energy required to lift a kilogram of apples from the ground to a table that is about a metre high.

James Prescott Joule (1818–1889) was an English scientist who also ran a very successful beer-brewing business. He studied the nature of heat and discovered its relationship to mechanical work. This led to the first law of thermodynamics, the **Law of Conservation of Energy.**

Source: Wikimedia Commons

*James Joule*

He had to manage the family business, so science could only be a (somewhat serious) hobby. Still, he kept conducting experiments and studying how energy changes forms. He was neither a professor nor an engineer, so he had a difficult time getting people to take his ideas seriously.

Joule devised experiments and concluded that 'wherever mechanical force is expended, an exact equivalent of heat is always obtained'. Initially, British scientists did not believe him, but with the help of more accurate thermometers, Joule proved that he was right. Mechanical energy does get converted to heat energy.

His gravestone has the number '772.55' etched in it. This is the amount of work in foot-pound units done at sea level that he calculated would raise the temperature of one pound of water from 60 to 61 degrees Fahrenheit.

The second law is the **Law of Increased Entropy,** which states that entropy – a scientific measure of disorderliness – inside any closed system always increases. This is why a glass that shatters into many pieces when it lands on the floor doesn't magically repair itself.

For centuries, scientists pondered over the possibility of inventing perpetual motion machines. Ever since human beings built the first machines, they dreamed of creating one that would work forever and on its own, without needing any energy supply. Such a machine would keep going on by itself. Imagine a pencil that never has to be sharpened, or a car that does not need petrol or batteries.

Of course such a thing is impossible because it would disobey the first and second laws of thermodynamics.

Because of the conservation of energy, we cannot create energy out of nothing. And while the machine functions, it will continuously be losing energy to its surroundings in the form of heat. So, it will finally run out of energy and stop at some point.

The third law of thermodynamics is the **Law of Entropy at Absolute Zero**. It states that the entropy of a system approaches a constant value as the temperature approaches absolute zero. One of the consequences of this law is that it is impossible for a closed system to attain a temperature of absolute zero.

Thermodynamics initially emerged from the desire to make steam engines more efficient. Today, its principles have far-reaching applications. Scientists use thermodynamics to design better cars and refrigerators, unravel the mysteries of outer space, enhance the properties of materials, and even enable chemists to predict the outcome of chemical reactions.

Physicists are also trying to combine thermodynamics with the ideas of quantum mechanics. We will talk about quantum mechanics in greater detail later in the book.

# 14

# Invisible Rays

Maxwell's ground-breaking equations had predicted the existence of electromagnetic waves – oscillating electric and magnetic fields travelling at the speed of light. It paved the way for our understanding of the spectrum. Visible light is one type of electromagnetic wave; scientists have since discovered many other types of waves that can be put in the same category. Today, we harness these waves for countless applications.

## Beyond Red

The term 'VIBGYOR' is used to describe the seven colours of light that we can see: violet, indigo, blue, green, yellow, orange and red. But light extends beyond what our eyes perceive. Infrared waves were the first rays beyond the visible spectrum to be discovered. While invisible to our eyes, we experience infrared waves every day, in the form of heat.

In the 1800s, the German-British scientist William Herschel carried out an experiment to study the different temperatures corresponding to the various colours of light. He placed thermometers within each colour of a visible spectrum. The results showed that the temperature increased as the colours moved towards red. Then he discovered that the region beyond red had an even higher temperature. This is how he detected the presence of infrared light.

Infrared light is emitted or absorbed by molecules when a change takes place in the way they rotate or vibrate. It has a wide variety of uses. We can use infrared illumination to observe people and animals at night, without getting detected ourselves. Infrared rays have a wavelength – the distance between two peaks of a wave – greater than that of visible light, and they can pass through dust and clouds without deviating. This is why it is used in astronomy, as it can penetrate through clouds and dusty regions and reveal undiscovered objects such as new planets and stars. We can also use infrared light to detect changing blood flow in our bodies.

And when we are changing TV channels using our remote controls, we are in fact using infrared rays to send a message to the TV set.

## Beyond Violet

Beyond the violet end of the visible spectrum lies ultraviolet (UV) light. Its wavelength is shorter than that of visible light. Although invisible to the human eye, some insects such as bumble bees and butterflies can see UV light and use it for navigation and finding food. Reindeers depend upon UV rays to spot lichens – little plants that are crucial to their diet. Certain birds can make out the difference between the males and females of their species using UV markers.

The sun is a source of UV radiation, some of which manages to penetrate the earth's atmosphere. This is what causes tanning of the skin if you stay out in the sun for a long time. It can also cause premature ageing of the skin as well as skin cancer in certain cases. Sunscreen lotions are used to protect ourselves from these harmful rays. These lotions work by absorbing, reflecting or scattering sunlight.

UV rays were first discovered by German scientist Johann Wilhelm Ritter in 1801. Inspired by Herschel's discovery of infrared rays, Ritter conducted experiments to find out if invisible light existed below the violet end of the spectrum as well. Silver chloride is a chemical that turns black when exposed to sunlight, so Ritter decided to measure the rate at which silver chloride reacted to different colours of light.

He used a glass prism in the path of sunlight to create a spectrum and then placed silver chloride in each colour of the spectrum. He found that blue light caused silver chloride to darken much more efficiently than red light could. Then he placed some silver chloride beyond the violet end of the spectrum and found that there was an intense reaction, showing that there were invisible rays present in this region. Ritter gave these rays the name 'chemical rays', which later came to be known as ultraviolet light or ultraviolet radiation.

We use UV light in a variety of ways. It helps us kill bacteria and viruses, to sterilize equipment and disinfect products and their containers. Scientists also use UV light to study atoms and to learn about warmer objects in space.

## The X Factor

Beyond the UV rays, we have X-rays. These rays have a very small wavelength and extremely high energy, and can pass through more objects than the other rays can. They pass through skin and fat with relative ease, while muscles offer some resistance. However, they cannot penetrate through bones. This property is precisely why we can see bones so clearly on X-ray plates.

X-rays were discovered by the German physicist Wilhelm Roentgen in 1895. It happened by accident while he was doing some experiments with electricity, which involved passing an electric current through Crookes tubes. A Crookes tube is a kind of tube that has two electrical points, positive and negative, and from which all air has been removed.

During his work, Roentgen noticed that some nearby photographic plates had gone foggy. To find out why this had happened, he put some black paper on the tube and switched on the current. At this point, a nearby screen coated with barium began to glow. He correctly figured out that some unknown rays were being produced inside the tube. Because of their mysterious nature, he named them X-rays. All across science and mathematics, the letter X has been traditionally used to denote unknown things.

X-rays are not generated only by some scientists on earth. It has been found that mysterious star-like objects in space, known as 'quasars', emit X-rays as well.

The main use of X-rays, as we all know, is in medicine. If you have fallen and got hurt, you place your injured arm or leg in front of an X-ray machine, with a piece of photographic film behind, to see if you have broken any bones. Another use of X-rays in medicine is the killing of cancer cells. But X-rays also kill healthy cells. This is the reason why they must be used with great caution.

X-rays are used at airports to check customers and their baggage, to make sure they are not carrying anything illegal or harmful. They are also used by art historians to find out more about how a painting was done and whether an old painting is genuine or a forgery. An X-ray study of a painting can show us how the artist began their painting and how they painted new colours, figures and layers over what they had originally done. This gives us a sense of what was going through the artist's mind as they painted. In some cases, it has even been found that the painting that we see today was done over a totally different earlier painting by the same artist.

*The Virgin of the Rocks* is one of Leonardo da Vinci's most famous paintings, depicting the Virgin Mary with the baby Jesus. We can see it at the National Gallery in London. Some years ago, using X-rays, the gallery discovered that the painting originally had a very different composition. In fact, da Vinci had painted it thrice, one over the other, with the same figures in different poses, and only the third and final version is visible to us through the naked eye.

X-rays are also used to find out the arrangement of atoms within a crystal. When a beam of X-rays strikes a crystal, it gets scattered in many different directions. By studying the angles and intensities of these scattered beams, we can gather information about the various atoms in the crystal. This is known as X-ray crystallography.

## Smallest and Fastest: Gamma Rays, Microwaves, Radio Waves

Gamma rays are electromagnetic waves with the shortest wavelengths and highest frequencies. The simplest description of 'frequency' is the number of waves that pass through a certain point in one second. All electromagnetic waves travel at the speed of light, and for any electromagnetic wave, the wavelength multiplied by the frequency gives us the speed of light – which is a constant. This means the shorter the wavelength, the higher the frequency. Gamma rays are associated with radioactivity, which is a phenomenon we will talk about in the next chapter.

Like X-rays, microwaves are a kind of invisible electromagnetic waves. They have a very high frequency and low energy, and have revolutionized our lives in many ways. When we are speaking to a friend using

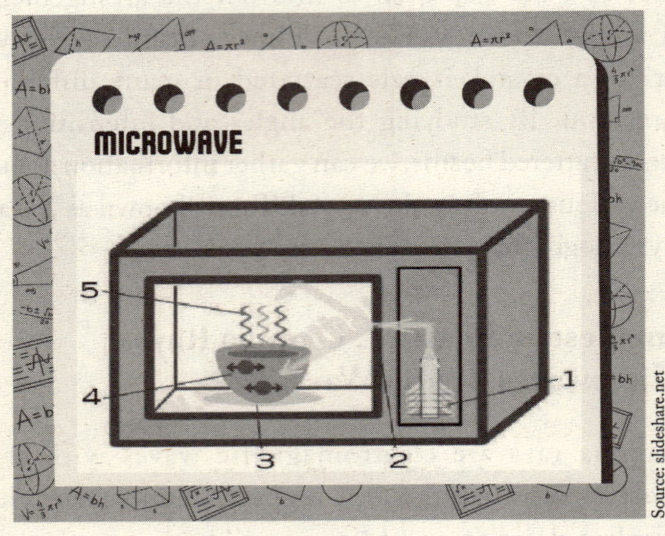


*How does your food get heated?*

*(1) Inside the box is a microwave generator called a magnetron that converts electricity into radio waves. (2) The magnetron directs waves into the food compartment through the wave guide. (3) The food sits on the turntable, spinning so that the waves cook it evenly. (4) The waves bounce back and forth off the reflective metal walls, passing into the food. As they travel through the food, they make the molecules vibrate. (5) The vibration causes the food to heat up.*

a cell phone, whether next door or thousands of miles away; using Google Maps to reach a place; listening to a song on FM radio in a car; using wi-fi to connect to the internet; or watching films on Netflix – we are using microwaves. And, of course, when we are heating up food in a ***microwave*** oven. So, we are dependent on microwave technology for a lot of things in our everyday life.

Microwaves also have medical as well as military uses. In medicine, they are used to study if anything is wrong inside the brain. In the military, they can be used to set off bombs in distant locations. The world's most powerful telescopes that gaze at the stars and galaxies billions of light years away and discover new things about our universe use microwaves and infrared waves instead of visible light.

James Clerk Maxwell, who had unified electromagnetism, had also predicted the existence of radio waves. Radio waves are electromagnetic radiation whose wavelengths extend from a fraction of a millimetre – many times smaller than a grain of rice – to hundreds of kilometres. The shortest ones are the microwaves, between a few millimetres and tens of centimetres in length. But they are still thousands of times longer than waves that make up the light that we can see.

Source: Wikimedia Commons

*James Clerk Maxwell*

In 1886, the German physicist Heinrich Hertz used Maxwell's theory to become the first person to transmit and receive controlled radio waves. The unit of frequency, the hertz, is named in his honour.

Very few Indians know that both wireless radio communication and microwave technologies were invented by **Jagadish Chandra Bose**, who was perhaps the greatest Indian scientist of the modern era. Bose was a man who firmly believed that he should not make money out of any of the work he did. He wanted everyone to be able to use the fruits of his inventions. That's why he refused to patent his inventions.

The Italian physicist Guglielmo Marconi is

today recognized worldwide as the inventor of radio communication. He received the Nobel Prize for Physics in 1909. Marconi was almost certainly aware of Bose's work and may have attended Bose's lectures in London, where he had explained his invention in detail. Being a very smart businessman in addition to being a scientist, he quietly borrowed some of Bose's work and told everyone that he had done it all on his own.

Bose never received the honours that he deserved. We tell the story of his life and achievements in Chapter 24.

**The Microwaved Chocolate**

The story of how the microwave oven was invented is quite interesting, though no one knows for sure if that is really how it happened.

During the Second World War, scientists were trying to develop better magnetrons to detect German warplanes. A magnetron emits microwaves that, when beamed out, can spot flying objects.

In 1945, a scientist named Percy Spencer at Raytheon, a major American company that makes advanced weapons, was working with magnetrons. He found that a candy bar he had in his pocket had melted.

Others had also seen that sort of thing happening but had not bothered to think about it. But Spencer was a curious man. He investigated and decided that this had happened due to the effect of microwaves.

He became convinced that microwaves could revolutionize cooking. He began experimenting with these waves on various types of food by putting them in a tightly shut metal box attached to a powerful microwave generator. This was the first oven, which produced the world's first microwaved popcorn. It also caused some pain to a co-worker when he opened the box and an egg inside it exploded in his face.

Spencer was paid just $2 by Raytheon for his invention: this is what the company paid its scientists for their inventions if the work had been done using the company's laboratories and money. However, the invention helped Spencer rise to a very high position in the company and become a wealthy man.

# 15

# Things That Glow in the Dark

Towards the end of the nineteenth century, scientists made an amazing discovery. They found that certain kinds of matter spontaneously emit certain rays and have always been doing so. They also found that the application of heat, light, electricity or any kind of force makes no difference to these emissions at all.

## Fluoro and Phospho

This important discovery, which took place on a cloudy day in 1896, was made by the French physicist Henri Becquerel (1852–1907). Becquerel had been born into a family of physicists and held the chair of applied physics at the National Museum of Natural History in Paris. In 1883, he got interested in fluorescence and phosphorescence.

What are fluorescence and phosphorescence? Certain substances absorb light or other electromagnetic radiation and then emit light themselves. In most cases, the emitted light has a longer wavelength and lower energy than the absorbed light. Fluorescence and phosphorescence are both processes which fall in this category. The main difference between the two phenomena is the length of time that they last. If the emission of light stops suddenly, it is fluorescence. If it lingers, it is phosphorescence. 'Glow in the dark' toys are phosphorescent.

Fluorescence and phosphorescence were areas in which Henri Becquerel's father had been an expert. Like his father, Henri was interested in uranium and its compounds. He was also an expert photographer.

In 1895, when Becquerel heard about Roentgen's discovery of X-rays, he began looking for a connection between the newly discovered invisible rays and phosphorescence. He tried experimenting with photographic plates and phosphorescent uranium salts by placing them in sunlight, thinking that the uranium salts might absorb sunlight and re-emit it as X-rays. He did get some results. Once, by chance, he placed the photographic plates and the uranium crystals in

*The discovery of radioactivity: Henri Becquerel had put some uranium crystals and photographic plates in a drawer. He found that the plates showed very clear images of the crystals and realized that uranium emits invisible rays.*

the same drawer. When he took out the plates and developed them, he saw a very clear image of the crystals. This showed him that the uranium crystals emitted invisible rays even in the dark.

At first, Becquerel thought that this was phosphorescence that lasted very long. However, he soon found that compounds of uranium that were non-phosphorescent also displayed the same property. His experiments led him to conclude that uranium, by itself, was radiating some kind of invisible rays. This was the first observation of **natural radioactivity**.

Many years later, this discovery would be used to make nuclear bombs.

## Alpha, Beta, Gamma

Marie Curie and Pierre Curie were both brilliant physicists. They were married to each other, and their partnership in science ushered in many important discoveries. Marie was of Polish origin; her maiden name was Maria Salomea Skłodowska. Pierre was French. In 1898, the Curies discovered radium and polonium while they were conducting research on the mineral known as pitchblende. Both of these are radioactive substances. Marie Curie named polonium after her motherland. In 1902, they were able to isolate radium salts from pitchblende. Marie Curie coined the term 'radioactivity'.

In 1903, Henri Becquerel and the Curies were awarded a joint Nobel Prize in physics for their original work in radioactivity. In 1911, Marie Curie was awarded a second Nobel Prize, this time in chemistry, for being

*Marie Curie*

able to isolate pure, metallic radium. She was the first person to win two Nobel Prizes.

Both 'becquerel' and 'curie' are today units of radioactivity. The becquerel is the International System of Units (SI) unit, which most of the world uses. The US uses the curie. One curie is equal to 37 billion becquerels.

After the discovery of radioactivity, physicists began to study the properties of the different types of radiations emitted by radioactive substances. Soon, they realized that radiation consisted of three kinds of rays. These were named 'alpha', 'beta' and 'gamma' rays.

Scientists were now able to explain radioactivity. They found that radioactivity occurs because some elements have unstable nuclei. The nucleus 'wants' to be stable and gives off radiation in the form of alpha, beta and gamma rays to reach a stable configuration. During this process the nucleus undergoes a change, and a different element is created. So we have what is known as **radioactive generations**. The polonium and radium that Pierre and Marie Curie extracted from pitchblende are direct descendants of uranium.

Ernest Rutherford had discovered that alpha particles, which make up alpha radiation, consist of two protons and two neutrons. When the nucleus has achieved too much mass, that is, it is overweight with almost an equal number of neutrons and protons, it emits an alpha particle to get lighter. This process, called 'alpha decay', makes the nucleus stable but, in the process, the atom changes to another element. For example, americium changes into neptunium when it goes through alpha decay.

Alpha decay usually takes place in heavy elements such as uranium, thorium, plutonium and radium. Out of the three – alpha, beta, gamma – alpha particles have the minimum penetrative power. Alpha rays are not harmful to humans if the source of radiation is outside the human body, because alpha particles cannot penetrate human skin. However, if the source is inside the body, the rays can have a bad effect.

When a nucleus contains an excess of neutrons (i.e., more neutrons than protons), it becomes unstable and emits beta rays, which are nothing but fast-moving electrons. This process is called beta decay, and it occurs to correct the imbalance between neutrons and protons. During beta decay, one of the neutrons transforms into a proton and an electron. The proton stays within the nucleus and the electron is thrown out. Thus, the number of neutrons decreases by one and the number of protons increases by one. This changes the atomic number of the element, resulting in the creation of a different element.

Because of their light mass, beta particles lose energy very quickly as they interact with matter and follow a zigzag path. They can penetrate only a few millimetres in materials and tens of centimetres through air. But they can be dangerous and any contact with our body must be avoided.

As we said in the last chapter, gamma rays are electromagnetic rays with very high frequencies. They have zero mass and the highest power of penetration. They can even pass through thick concrete. Gamma rays are used to sterilize medical equipment and food, as tracers in medicine that draw a picture of what is going inside our bodies, and in radiotherapy to kill cancerous cells. Astronomers use gamma rays to study the far corners of the universe. But they are also extremely dangerous and have to be handled with great care.

## Useful but Risky

Through experimental observation, scientists found that although radioactivity seems to be a random process, it is governed by a mathematical law of decay. Rutherford and his young student Frederick Soddy derived this law. There was a constant that appeared in the equation. They called this the **half-life.**

Suppose you take a radioactive element. The time taken by half of it to decay and transform into other elements is known as the half-life of the element. The half-life does not depend upon the amount of substance taken, or the temperature or pressure. The half-life of an element is one of its basic properties.

Like all human technologies, using radioactivity has many benefits, but it can also be harmful. Nuclear technology, which is based on radioactivity, can produce cheap and non-polluting electricity, but it can also be used to make bombs that can kill millions in a few minutes.

Today, radiation is a common and valuable tool in medicine, research and industry. But it is important to remember that exposure to large doses of radiation in a short period of time causes serious health effects and even death. In such cases, the intense radiation can overwhelm a human cell's ability to repair itself, ultimately leading to cell death. The effects can be far-reaching, with potential health issues even manifesting in children born years after their parents' exposure.

Marie Curie died of a certain type of anaemia, which almost certainly developed from her long hours of exposure to various radioactive substances, without taking any of the precautions that we now know are absolutely necessary. Nearly 90 years after she passed away, her papers and even her recipe book are still emitting radioactive rays. In fact, they will stay radioactive for another 1,500 years. Though her papers are considered a national treasure in France, they are stored in lead-lined boxes at the National Library in Paris. Those who wish to open the boxes must wear protective clothing and sign a legal document that if anything happens to them, it will be their own responsibility.

If the history of science teaches us anything, it's that all discoveries and inventions demand careful consideration. We must strive not only to improve life but also to safeguard against potential negative consequences. Science is a double-edged sword.

### The Radium Girls

The case of the 'Radium Girls' highlighted the dangers associated with radiation. There were women workers in some factories in America whose job was to paint watch dials with radium. The radium would help people see the time on their watches even when they were in a place that was pitch-dark. Although the management of the company suspected that the rays emitted by radium might have harmful effects on the human body, they did not take any necessary precautions. The girls were actually told by the company, United States Radium Corporation, to lick the brushes to make them pointy. This saved time and money for the company.

Many of the girls died from exposure to radiation. This terrible practice continued for many years, till five of the girls went to court against the company. In 1928, while the case was still being heard, the company agreed to pay the girls a large lumpsum amount, a regular amount every year for the rest of their lives, and to cover all their legal and medical expenses.

This was a great victory for the workers against a giant corporation. It also led to changes in laws across the world about companies making sure that they provide working conditions that do not affect their workers' health.

# 16

# The Music of Waves

Almost everything in nature creates some sort of sound. Sounds can be pleasant, like music. Sounds can also be irritating, like traffic noise. Music was created by ancients all over the world. Hymns to the gods have been chanted in places of worship and in homes for thousands of years. The mythologies and histories of all civilizations have references to music. In India, we have Lord Krishna's flute and the veena of Saraswati, the goddess of knowledge. The Greek epic Iliad was written to be sung to the accompaniment of a four-stringed lyre. Homer, the legendary Greek poet and author of the Iliad and the Odyssey, is often pictured as blind man with a lyre performing his immortal song to an audience. In the Bible, the great warrior-king David played the harp and has been described as a 'sweet singer'.

In fact, the word 'music' comes from the Muses, the daughters of Zeus, who was the king of the ancient Greek gods. The Muses were supposed to be the patron goddesses of all creative work.

Before modern scientists came into the picture, little was known about the nature of sound and how it travelled.

Aristotle, the Greek philosopher who keeps cropping up in our book, suggested that sound consists of waves that propagate in air through the motion of air particles. This was correct. However, this hypothesis was based on philosophy rather than actual evidence. He also thought

– wrongly – that high frequencies of sound travel faster than low frequencies.

This wrong assumption persisted for many centuries. Like in many other areas of science, Galileo was the first person who studied sound scientifically. Interest in sound came naturally, since he was a talented musician. He experimentally found out the correlation between pitch and frequency of the sound source – the higher the frequency, the sharper the sound. After the foundational work done by Galileo, there was rapid progress in the field of acoustics.

**Acoustics** is the field of physics that studies sound. It gets its name from the Greek word 'akouein', which means 'hear'.

## The Speed of Sound

Marin Mersenne, a seventeenth-century French polymath, is known as the father of acoustics. He was the first person to study the vibration of stretched strings, such as in a piano or violin, in a systematic and scientific manner. He discovered a beautiful law connecting the pitch to the tension, length and thickness of a vibrating string. In his book *Harmonie Universelle,* he put together discussions on music, sound and experimental science. This formed the basis of modern acoustics. Using echoes, he gave a reasonably accurate estimate of the speed of sound. The precision was quite remarkable, considering that there were no sophisticated instruments at that time.

Our next hero is Robert Boyle, the British scientist who appeared in our chapter on heat. Boyle stated and proved that a medium was necessary for sound waves to propagate. To demonstrate that sound cannot travel through a vacuum, he conducted an experiment in which he placed a ringing bell inside a glass jar. Then he slowly pumped out air from the glass jar and observed that when all the air had been removed, the ringing noise made by the bell could no longer be heard. This proved his hypothesis that a material medium is necessary for the propagation of sound.

Newton gave us the first known theoretical treatise on sound in his *Principia Mathematica.* He predicted a value for the speed of sound in air, which is about 15 per cent different from the value that is accepted today. Early values of the speed were obtained by measurement of the time it took for the cannon shots to cover a given distance.

Nearly 150 years later, in 1826, scientists carried out experiments under the waters of Lake Geneva in

Switzerland. They took measurements and found a value only 0.2 per cent below the value that is accepted today.

The speed of sound is about 343 metres per second if it is moving through a medium of air of normal density at 20 degrees Celsius. The speed is dependent on temperature as well as the medium through which it is moving. At 0 degree Celsius, which is the freezing point of water, the speed is about 331 metres per second.

As we all know, today we have many types of aircraft, especially fighter jets, that travel faster than sound.

## The Medium Is the Music

Through the 1700s and 1800s, substantial research was conducted on sound waves. The French mathematician Joseph Fourier discovered that the sound waves produced by vibrating strings are just a series of waves that ebbed and flowed according to a set pattern.

Austrian physicist Christian Doppler made some very important discoveries about the frequency of sound waves – that the frequency of the waves, as heard by the listener, is altered if the source of sound moves closer or farther away. He found that when the source is moving away from the listener, the frequency becomes lower and when it is moving towards the observer, the listener hears a higher pitch.

If you are on the road in a car and an ambulance or a fire engine comes by, with its siren on, moving fast and overtaking the car you are in, you hear the siren as high-pitched as it comes towards you, and then the pitch lowers as it speeds away from you. This is known as the **Doppler Effect.**

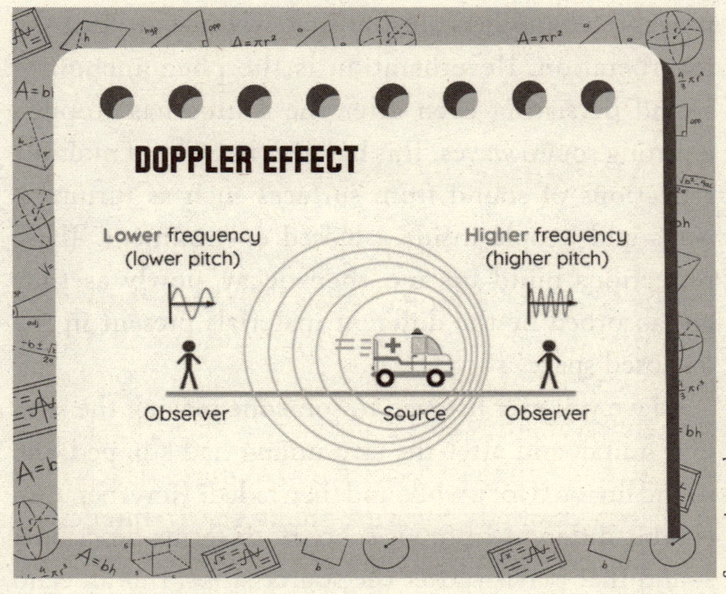

Source: scienceready.com.au

Doppler developed a mathematical equation for the frequency of sound when there is relative motion between the source of sound and the listener.

## What, but Also Where

Wallace Sabine, who was a physicist at Harvard University, made an important discovery relating to sound and music in the late 1890s. Before Sabine, nobody had really bothered about the venue musicians played in.

Sabine was tasked with renovating and improving the acoustics of a Harvard museum. During this process, Sabine became the first scientist to measure reverberation. Reverberation is the phenomenon of sound persisting even after the source has stopped emitting sound waves. This happens because of multiple reflections of sound from surfaces such as furniture, walls and people inside a closed environment. These reflections build up and then decay slowly as they get absorbed by the different materials present in the enclosed space.

Have you ever listened to someone playing the sitar or a guitar, and after the strumming had stopped, the sound lingered for a while and then faded? Reverberation is a bit different from an echo. Both terms describe a sound that persists after the source stops. But an echo is the distinct reflection of the exact noise – you shout 'hello hello' to a rocky mountain and the mountain replies 'hello hello' back. In reverberation, the sound waves bounce off surfaces, causing a muddied repetition of the original sound. Different materials absorb sound differently. A heavy cotton curtain absorbs sound much more than, say, a wooden or brick wall.

Sabine conducted various experiments with the seats of the venue and different materials that absorb sound. The Boston Symphony Hall became the first building that was constructed taking acoustics into account. Today, whenever a concert hall is built, a lot of attention is paid to acoustics. It is because of Sabine's work that we get to hear the beautiful quality of music in concert halls.

**Raman and Mridangam**

The great Indian scientist C.V. Raman, who won the Nobel Prize for Physics in 1930 (more on him in Chapter 23), was deeply interested in acoustics. He spent many years studying the physics of the sound produced by two Indian percussion instruments, the mridangam and the tabla, curious about their 'remarkable acoustic principles'.

In 1919, he started a series of experiments on the mridangam, an instrument that is at least 2,000 years old. In 1935, he explained why the mridangam and the tabla produced such consistent sound and music. The drumhead that stretches over the wooden shell is carefully loaded with a mixture of iron oxide, charcoal, starch and gum. The rigid shell of the mridangam increases the energy of the vibrations set off by the beating of the drumhead. The shell also has a large amount of compressed air which adds to the instrument's harmony.

In fact, Raman found that the mridangam uses complex theories of physics. The drumhead has three layers of skin and 16 tension equalizers. This is to ensure that it does not tear and vibrates properly to produce exactly the sound that an expert player wants from it.

In 1921, when Raman was in England, he studied how sound travels in the Whispering Gallery of the dome of St Paul's Cathedral in London, where your whispers are heard clearly by others at the other end of a vast hall.

You can have the same experience in the Golconda Fort in Hyderabad, where the sound of a clap can travel more than 1 kilometre inside the citadel through a clever mix of building materials and many scientifically designed arches that help carry the sound through the air.

# 17

# Einstein and a Whole New World

What comes to your mind when you hear the name Albert Einstein? The picture of a man with wild hair, his tongue sticking out? That iconic photograph was probably a joke. Or maybe he was annoyed with pesky photographers. But what the photo reveals is that he had a free spirit and little regard for convention.

If you think about it, science would not have progressed if scientists were boring, conventional people. Scientists dare to question established conventions; they use their imagination, logic, mathematics and all their intuitive powers to understand how nature works. Einstein was one such hero and is regarded as one the two greatest physicists ever. The other is Newton, of course.

## The World Becomes a Mystery

By the time Einstein started his work, physics had settled down to some degree. Newton's theories were regarded as the ultimate truth. There were a few doubts here and there, but everyone was quite satisfied with Newtonian physics. What Einstein discovered shook the world. He did not disprove Newtonian physics but offered a more expansive general theory that would explain our universe in a new and more complete way.

Before Einstein came into the picture, classical mechanics had developed to the point that it could explain complex macroscopic phenomena – things and events that you could see with your eyes.

Source: Wikimedia Commons

*Albert Einstein*

Thermodynamics was a well-established field. Kinetic theory could explain the behaviour of gases. Physicists had studied electricity and magnetism and had come to understand that light consisted of electromagnetic waves. The laws of conservation of mass and energy were widely accepted.

So much had been achieved that people assumed that all the important laws of physics had been discovered. However, around the 1900s, some physicists began to have doubts about whether classical theories were enough to explain the workings of the universe. There were certain phenomena that classical physics could just not explain.

Take black body radiation, for instance. A 'black body' is an object that absorbs all the light that falls on it. It does not reflect or transmit light. However, it does produce heat radiation. The energy distribution of the emitted radiation depends only on the temperature of the black body. Classical physics, as well as common sense, would suggest that the intensity of emission would increase with an increase in the frequencies of the waves. However, it was seen that at very high frequencies, the intensity was, in fact, lower. Scientists were at a loss to explain why this was so.

Another example is the photoelectric effect. When light shines on a metal, electrons are sometimes ejected from its surface. This is known as the photoelectric effect. But these electrons were being thrown out the instant light fell on them, with no time lag. Moreover, the speed of the ejected electrons seemed to have nothing to do with the intensity of the light that was shone on the metals. These observations contradicted the laws of Newtonian physics, which had been proven true in the macroscopic world.

There were other discoveries, too, that no one could explain. We have talked about the discovery of X-rays by Roentgen, radioactivity by Becquerel, and new radioactive elements by Marie and Pierre Curie. All these discoveries led scientists to question the supposed indestructibility of the atom and the nature of matter. Ernest Rutherford had found experimental evidence that the atom consists of a dense, positively charged nucleus surrounded by negatively charged electrons. However, classical theory predicted that such a structure would be unstable.

A massive challenge to classical physics came from the **Michelson-Morley experiment**. It was performed in 1887 by American scientists Albert A. Michelson and Edward W. Morley. The experiment found something that defied the established laws of physics – that the speed of light did not change whether the light travelled *with* the earth or *against* the earth's motion. That is, the speed of light remained constant, irrespective of the motion of the source or the observer.

These discoveries demanded a new explanation. And the search for these answers would lead to the birth of quantum mechanics and relativity.

## The Boy Who Didn't Speak

In his childhood, Einstein did not display any signs of brilliance. In fact, his parents were worried because he learnt to speak rather late. They took him to doctors, but the doctors could find nothing wrong with the child.

There are two stories about the first words that Einstein spoke. Both are possibly untrue.

In one, he was two-and-a-half years old when his parents brought his baby sister to him to play with her. Little Albert asked: **'Yes, but where are its wheels?'** The other story goes that Albert didn't speak a word until he was three or four years old. Then suddenly, during supper one night, he said, 'The soup is too hot.' His parents were hugely relieved and asked him why he had never spoken a word till then. 'Because,' replied Albert, 'until now, everything has been fine.'

Einstein also did not excel in school. He graduated with a degree in teaching but found it hard to get a job. Finally, he obtained the post of a clerk at the patent office in Berne in Switzerland in 1902. But the seven years that he worked there turned out to be the most fruitful years of his life. There was not much work in the office, so he could spend most of his time pondering over all the puzzling questions of physics. There, he came up with many radical ideas.

The year 1905 was a big one for Einstein, who was then only 26 years old. Four of his papers were published in the *German Yearbook of Physics*. Three of them amazed the world of science. The first was on Brownian motion. Brownian motion is the random movement of particles in a gas or a liquid that occurs when the particles are hit by fast-moving atoms or molecules. It was first discovered by Robert Brown in 1827. Einstein, in his paper, gave a detailed mathematical description of this motion. This was a huge step forward in physics. It also convinced many scientists that atoms and molecules really did exist and were not merely theoretical entities.

His second paper was on the photoelectric effect. Einstein used the ideas of quantum mechanics developed by German physicist Max Planck to explain the phenomenon. He used the concept of quanta or packets of energy and was able to explain the photoelectric effect. In 1921, Einstein received the Nobel Prize for this paper.

His third paper is his most famous one, on the

Theory of Special Relativity. This theory starts with two basic assumptions. The first is that the speed of light is constant; the second is that the laws of physics are the same for all inertial **frames of reference**.

## It All Depends . . .

The concept of 'frame of reference' lies at the heart of 'relativity'.

Here's a simple example. Let's say you are standing on the roadside when a car goes by at 30 km/hour. You see it going past at that speed.

But if you are in a car moving at 30 km/hour, and there is another car next to yours that is also moving exactly at the same speed, your frame of reference would tell you that neither car is moving at all. Indeed, aircraft can do air-to-air refuelling by matching speeds so that they are not moving in relation to each other, even though both aircraft may be flying at 500 km/hour in relation to the earth's surface.

Or, imagine you are in a car that is going at 60 km/hour, and you overtake a car that's moving at 30 km/hour. Your frame of reference about that car will be different once again, and you will actually see the other car going *backwards* at 30 km/hour.

When translated into cosmological terms, frames of reference can throw up very strange effects. The earth is stationary to somebody standing on his balcony. Yet, the earth is moving at 107,000 km/hour in its orbit around the sun, and the entire solar system is also moving through space at a mind-boggling 720,000 km/hour.

A spaceship moving through space very far away from the effects of the gravity of stars and galaxies would be the ultimate example of an unusual frame of reference. Using such assumptions, some mathematics and large doses of imagination (which he called thought experiments), Einstein arrived at some really shocking conclusions.

The most important one was that the Newtonian belief that space and time were fundamentally different things was wrong. The moment you take the speed of light to be constant, wherever you are and however fast you are moving, space and time get linked.

The classic thought experiment is that of two twin sisters. One stays on earth and the other goes off in a rocket that moves close to the speed of light to reach a star that is 10 light years away. Time travels 10 times slower on the rocket than on earth. So when the astronaut returns after travelling 20 light years, she is only 2 years older, but her earth twin has aged 20 years!

Einstein also found that mass and energy are interrelated, and one can be converted into the other! This led to the most famous equation in the history of physics, **E = MC²**. The amount of energy that a piece of matter contains – whether it's a clump of mud or a tiny bit of a radioactive element – is equal to the mass of that object multiplied by the speed of light multiplied again by the speed of light.

Because the speed of light is such a big number – 300,000 km/second, even a tiny amount of mass is equivalent to, and can be converted into, a very large amount of energy. This is why nuclear power is so useful and atomic bombs are so powerful.

## Space and Time

Einstein knew that there were some loopholes in his Theory of Relativity. It could not be reconciled with Newton's law of gravity, which was obviously correct. So, in 1915, he proposed the Theory of General Relativity, which explained that his Theory of Special Relativity did not contradict gravitational laws; the two were sides of the same coin.

He proposed that space and time became curved around massive objects. Instead of just being an invisible force that attracts objects to one another, as found by

Newton, **gravity warps space**. The more massive an object, the more it warps the space around it. For example, the sun is huge enough to warp space across our solar system. That is why our earth and other planets move in curved paths around it, called orbits.

This warping also affects the measurements of time. We tend to think of time as ticking away at a steady rate. But just as gravity can warp space, it can also stretch time. Suppose there is a mountain on earth that is 5 million feet high, and your friend somehow manages to climb to the top. You will clearly see that his clock is ticking faster than the one you are looking at, sitting in Mumbai or Chennai. We actually see such time-dilation effects when calculating time at an international space station, versus time on earth, because of such relativistic effects.

This is due to the difference in the strength of gravity at different places. In our real life on our planet earth, the watches that we wear are not sensitive enough to show this. After all, our highest mountain peak, Mount Everest, is just around 29,000 feet high.

In 1919, the British astronomer Arthur Eddington led a team to the island of Principe, off the west coast of Africa, to take measurements during a total solar eclipse. The photographs they took showed that light was bending around the sun, proving this part of the Theory of General Relativity to be true.

Einstein became an overnight star. This grand discovery also came at a time when the people of Europe were so exhausted after the First World War that they needed something new and interesting to hold on to. Einstein's achievement gave them what they needed. Newspapers hailed him as the new Newton, and he travelled the world, giving lectures on his theories about the cosmos.

By the 1920s, Einstein had made all his important contributions to physics. Although he was an early pioneer in studying quantum mechanics in the photoelectric effect, he never fully believed in quantum mechanics. He would have lengthy debates with his friend, the Danish physicist Niels Bohr. These debates helped Bohr refine his own concepts. In later years, Einstein spent his time looking for a Unified Field Theory – one grand equation that would explain all the forces of nature. He also wrote on various other topics, particularly on world peace.

In 1952, the Republic of Israel offered him its presidency. He refused. In his letter of refusal, he wrote: 'All my life I have dealt with objective matters, hence I lack both the natural aptitude and the experience to deal properly with people and to exercise official functions.'

Einstein was certainly the greatest physicist of the twentieth century, and there is no scientist in the world who has been so famous and respected and loved by the common people, even though most of them could not make much sense of his discoveries.

### An Interesting Life

Einstein fell in love with physics in his childhood when his father gifted him a compass. He would spend hours studying the way the magnets moved inside the compass. Years later, this would help him develop his theories of relativity.

He was a **'bad boy'** in school: he hated the strict discipline and left when he was 15. After that, he applied to the Swiss Federal Polytechnic School in Zürich, Switzerland, and failed the entrance exam, but was still admitted because he had scored perfect marks in the math paper. But he remained a 'bad' student, bunking classes. His professors did not give him a good recommendation when he graduated, so he could only get the job of a clerk, which required hardly any use of his brain.

But this proved to be a boon because he could finish his daily work in a couple of hours and study more physics. When his first marriage broke up, as part of the divorce settlement in 1919, he agreed to give his wife, Mileva Maric (who was a gifted mathematician herself) all the money he might receive from the Nobel Prize, which he was very confident of winning. He did so when he won the prize two years later.

He left Germany forever in 1933 to settle in America just before Hitler came to power. Since he was Jewish, his books were burnt in Germany by the Nazis. When the Second World War broke out, he wrote to US President Franklin D. Roosevelt, urging him to begin research on a nuclear bomb because he had heard that Germany was doing so.

Einstein himself had no role to play in the American government's project to build a **nuclear bomb**, but after he saw the huge destruction of the Japanese cities of Hiroshima and Nagasaki caused by the bombs dropped by the US, he deeply regretted his advice to Roosevelt. In fact, he became the world's most famous advocate for banning nuclear weapons, pleading with governments to 'find peaceful means for the settlement of all disputes between them'.

# 18

# Does God Play Dice?

Remember when we said that if relativity was weird, quantum mechanics is weirder? Here is what some of the great thinkers of the twentieth century had to say about quantum mechanics: '**Quantum mechanics makes absolutely no sense**,' said Sir Roger Penrose, one of the finest British mathematicians ever. Einstein, too, refused to believe in its concepts, saying, 'God does not play dice.' He also said, 'If it [quantum mechanics] is correct, it signifies the end of physics as a science.' Even Erwin Schrodinger, who was in fact one of the founders of this branch of physics said, 'I do not like it, and I am sorry I ever had anything to do with it.'

## The Road to Uncertainty

Quantum mechanics provides a mathematical framework for the description and behaviour of sub-atomic particles, such as neutrons, protons, electrons, quarks and gluons. Till now, more than 200 types of sub-atomic particles have been detected, most of them highly unstable, some existing for less than a millionth of a second.

We had briefly mentioned black body radiation in the last chapter. The great German physicist Max Planck was studying this phenomenon. Black body radiation is radiation emitted by a body that is a 'perfect emitter'. It does not reflect or transmit the light energy that falls on it. It only absorbs the energy and then emits it. Experimentally, it was found that the emitted radiation is not related to what the black body is made up of and only depends on its temperature.

Planck did his calculations and found that the experimental results could be justified only if one assumed that energy is distributed in little packets, or 'discrete quanta', as they are called. **Quanta** are the smallest units of energy that can be transferred or exchanged in physical processes. However, the existence of quanta went against Newtonian physics, which had concluded that energy was a continuous flow, like a river or a sea. Yet, Planck was saying that it was like bullets being fired all the time.

Niels Bohr then created a new model for an atom, one that would explain Planck's observations. Like earlier models, here too, a positively charged nucleus was at the centre of an atom with electrons orbiting around it. Logic dictates that electrons orbiting around the nucleus would be governed by the same laws that cause planets to orbit around the sun. However, Bohr put forward an entirely different theory.

Source: Wikimedia Commons

*Niels Bohr*

He stated that around each atomic nucleus, there were several levels of concentric shells, inside which the electrons moved. Electrons could jump from one shell to another. After studying the light emitted by hydrogen atoms, Bohr concluded that atoms radiate light only when an electron jumps from an outer shell to one closer to the nucleus. The energy lost by the electron is the energy of the quantum of light emitted.

German physicist Werner Heisenberg objected to this description of the atom. He said that since these orbits around the nucleus could not be observed, they were imaginary. Instead, he tried to develop a mathematical model that would describe phenomena that were observable. He came up with 'matrix mechanics', which was a new kind of mathematics. Matrix mechanics led him to discover a strange effect that we know today as the **Heisenberg Uncertainty Principle**. It states that, for sub-atomic particles, one can either know where it is located or how fast it is moving, but not both at the same time.

This sounds like a very difficult concept, but let us give an example from the world that we can see, hear and sense. Let's say you and your friend both have smartphones with cameras whose shutter speeds – how long the camera records your subject – can be adjusted. Now suppose both of you are in the stadium in an Indian Premier League match where Mahendra Singh Dhoni is keeping wickets for Chennai Super Kings. The batman edges a ball that goes flying about 8 feet to the right of Dhoni. **Dhoni leaps sideways** and of course he catches it. Both of you have clicked your cameras as MSD was in the air. Your shutter speed is set at 1/30th of a second while your friend's is set at one second.

Your photo will catch Dhoni in mid-air – a clear shot – and it will show his exact position at that instant of time. But it will give no clue about Dhoni's speed. Your friend's photo, however, will be slightly blurred, because Dhoni would have flown several feet in that one second. His photo will accurately depict how fast Dhoni lunged at that ball, but it will be unable to give any precise information about where he was at any instant.

Here you and your friend were the observers, and MSD was the electron. Neither of the cameras can capture the full picture in one photo.

## The Undead Cat

There were more twists and turns to come. Austrian physicist Erwin Schrodinger proposed an entirely different quantum theory. He said that the electron is not a particle, but a wave function spread through space. It means that if you take an exact location, you cannot say that the electron is definitely there. There is only a *probability* of it being there, which can be calculated. It took people some time to believe this, but it was shown later that Heisenberg's approach and Schrodinger's approach were both correct. Paul Dirac, another great physicist, showed that we can derive Heisenberg and Schrodinger from the same mathematical equation. An electron is both a particle and a wave at once!

To reconcile the dual behaviour of fundamental particles, Bohr introduced the concept of complementarity to physics. He stated that all fundamental particles have a wave nature and a particle nature at the same time, and both the pictures must be taken into account for a complete description of sub-atomic particles. Depending on the experimental arrangement, one observes either wave-like properties or particle-like properties. However, it is not possible to observe both aspects simultaneously.

So we can know only the *probability*, which is a wave, of an electron moving at a specific speed or its location.

But what happens when two probability waves overlap? Like waves of water, they form a more complex pattern. The math shows that when an electron is caught in this overlap, it can be moving at two different speeds or be in two different places at the same time. This is like a coin being heads up and tails up at the same time and is known as quantum superposition.

**'Schrodinger's Cat'** is a very famous thought experiment about quantum superposition. In the experiment, Schrodinger asks you to imagine a cat locked up in a box which has a small amount of radioactive element and a Geiger counter that measures the amount of radioactive decay. There is a 50 per cent chance that the radioactive element may decay. Which means there is also a 50 per cent chance that it may not.

If the radioactive substance decays, it triggers the Geiger counter which causes a poison to be released that kills the cat. We cannot see what's happening inside the box, so we have no way of knowing whether the cat is dead or alive at a certain moment. Therefore, until we open the box and check, the cat is both dead and alive at the same time! Yes, this sounds absurd in our world, but the theory applies only at the level of sub-atomic particles. At that level, a thing exists only when we observe it. A sub-atomic particle is just a mathematical possibility, and it becomes a 'real' thing only when we go looking for it.

Of course this is all very weird stuff that totally defies what we call common sense. But all the high-level math that quantum physicists have worked with for more than a century suggests that this is how it is down there. There have been many experiments that verify the predictions of these strange theories and all our electronics – from televisions to space telescopes – depends on quantum theory. These wave-cum-particles that behave in such a seemingly illogical manner make up everything that we see up here in our 'normal' world.

### When Is an Electron an Electron?

The Solvay Conference on Quantum Mechanics, held in Brussels in 1927, was perhaps the most important meeting of physicists ever. Of the 29 scientists who attended, 17 had either already received or would receive Nobel prizes.

The conference marked the beginning of one of the great battles in the history of physics, between two great figures, Niels Bohr and Albert Einstein. Both had by then won Nobel Prizes. But they disagreed sharply on the way the universe worked.

Bohr's theory was that a quantum particle like an electron does not exist in one state or another but in all its possibilities at once. The idea of the particle becomes a real electron only when **someone observes it.** The act of observation **causes** its existence. In Bohr's words, the particles have no 'independent reality in the ordinary physical sense'.

Einstein rejected this theory. An electron is an electron, he said, and it will always be there even if no one is looking at it. For some 30 years, till Einstein passed away in 1955, he and Bohr would argue with each other on this, both in private and public. 'God does not play dice,' Einstein famously said. 'Stop telling God what to do,' was Bohr's reply. However, the two men respected each other deeply and their debates were always very civil.

As of now, Bohr seems to be the winner of the argument the two had.

# 19

# It Doesn't Matter

We have seen in the last two chapters how Einstein changed our entire view of space and time and how the discovery of quantum physics made us really stretch our imagination. But there were more peculiar discoveries to be made. Antimatter was one.

## Adventures in a Balloon

In 1911 and 1912, the Austrian physicist Victor Franz Hess undertook a series of rides in a hot air balloon to the upper layers of the atmosphere. These were dangerous flights, and if something went wrong, Hess could have died.

Hess was looking for a source of ionizing radiation.

This is a form of energy that acts by removing electrons from atoms and molecules of material that include air, water, and living tissue. According to what physicists knew at that time, it was logical to believe that the levels of ionizing radiation in the earth's atmosphere would decrease as the distance from the earth increased. So it did, but at higher altitudes in the atmosphere, it again increased and to levels higher than those on the ground. This phenomenon baffled scientists for many years.

Hess decided to solve this mystery. First, he built extremely sensitive electroscopes – instruments that detect and measure electricity. He then took them high up in the atmosphere in the balloon and noted down the readings. He carefully measured the radiation at altitudes of up to 5.3 kilometres (where it must have been very difficult to breathe!).

In 1911, Hess's balloon reached an altitude of around 1,100 metres, but he found no significant change in the amount of radiation as compared to the ground level. So the source of radiation could not be rocks. In 1912, Hess went up to a height of 5,300 metres in his balloon during a near-total eclipse of the sun. The ionization did not decrease during the solar eclipse. Hess concluded that the sun was not the source of radiation either. The radiation came from further out in space. In fact, Hess had discovered **cosmic rays** – high-energy sub-atomic particles that rain down on the earth from outside the solar system at nearly the speed of light.

In the late 1930s, like many other great Jewish scientists, writers and painters based in Germany and Austria, Hess migrated to America to escape Nazi persecution. By then he was already a Nobel laureate, having won it for his discovery.

## The Problem with Two Solutions

In the last two chapters we have spoken about how quantum theory and Einstein's Special Theory of Relativity came into being. In 1928, the British physicist Paul Dirac wrote an equation that united quantum theory and special relativity. This equation could be used to describe the behaviour of an electron moving at a speed close to the speed of light. It also incorporated Einstein's theory of relativity in the study of atoms. Today, the **Dirac Equation** is considered to be one of the most important equations in physics.

However, there was an obvious problem with the equation when Dirac formulated it. It was mathematically perfect but had two possible solutions, sort of like a high-level quadratic equation. In one

Source: Wikimedia Commons

*Paul Dirac*

solution, the electron would have negative energy, and in the other, it would have positive energy. How could that be? It was by now well-established that electrons had a negative charge.

Dirac explained this by proposing that for every particle in the universe there exists a corresponding antiparticle, which is identical to the particle but has an opposite charge. He stated that it was by accident that the earth and the solar system had negative electrons and positive protons. Maybe there were other star systems that have positive electrons and negative protons. So instead of matter as we know it, they are made up of **antimatter**. He won the Nobel Prize in 1932 along with Erwin Schrodinger of the cat-in-the-box fame.

## The Upside-Down World

In 1932, only a year after Dirac had published his theory of antimatter, Carl Anderson, a young professor at the California Institute of Technology (CalTech) in the US, was studying showers of cosmic particles in a cloud chamber. A cloud chamber is a particle detector. It is a container with saturated vapour inside. When a charged particle passes through the vapour, the vapour gets ionized and the particle produces a trail inside, which is much like the trail made by a jet plane as it moves through a cloud.

To his amazement, he found tracks left by positively charged particles with the same mass as electrons. After a year of careful observation, he concluded that these particles were antielectrons, the existence of which had been predicted by Dirac. The impact of the cosmic rays in the cloud chamber had produced pairs of electrons and antielectrons. He named the newly discovered particle 'positron'.

The discovery of the positron created a big buzz in the world of physics. Physicists began looking for the antiproton, a particle with the same mass as a proton but negatively charged. In 1954, Ernest Lawrence supervised the building of a proton accelerator named the Bevatron at the University of Berkeley, California. The machine's name comes from BeV, which was the symbol used for 'billion electron-volt' at that time. Inside the Bevatron, protons were made to strike the nuclei of a metal at extremely high speeds. This released enormous energy, which produced a new proton. But it was found that every such proton had a twin – an antiproton. The anti-proton would be destroyed almost as soon as it appeared. But appear, it did.

'Observation of Anti-protons' was the title of a paper published in the November 1955 issue of the journal *Physical Review Letters*, written by Berkeley scientists working with the Bevatron. The paper announced the detection of a new sub-atomic particle, which was identical to a proton, except that it had a negative charge. Owen Chamberlain and Emilio Segrè were awarded the Nobel Prize in Physics in 1959 for their discovery. Lawrence had already won it in 1939 for building the world's first cyclotron, which is what particle accelerators were called then.

Soon antineutrons were produced from antiprotons by a second team working with the Bevatron. Antineutrons were produced by passing a beam of antiprotons through matter. By the early 1960s, it became clear that electrons, protons and neutrons each had corresponding antiparticles. The next question that arose was this: Would antiprotons, positrons and antineutrons combine to form antiatoms, the basic component of antimatter? Also, are matter and antimatter exactly equal and opposite – in other words, 'symmetric' – as Dirac had predicted?

## Fearful Symmetry

How could we find out if this symmetry really existed? Physicists were also eager to learn how matter and antimatter would behave when brought together. Would antiprotons and antineutrons combine to form antinuclei? The answers to these questions were found in 1965, when the antideuteron was discovered.

Isotopes are forms of elements that are slightly different at the atomic level. Like many other elements, hydrogen has several isotopes with slightly different atomic compositions. An element always has the same number of protons, so the atomic number of an element is always the same. Hydrogen has an atomic number of 1, for example. However, an element may have different numbers of neutrons, which is why isotopes differ by atomic mass.

A deuteron is the nucleus of what is called 'heavy hydrogen' or deuterium. It has one proton and one neutron and is sometimes called hydrogen-2 since it has an atomic mass of 2. The nucleus of the much more common form of hydrogen has only a proton and no neutron.

The discovery of the antideuteron, made up of an antiproton and an antineutron, was simultaneously made by two teams of physicists – one working at CERN, the European Organization for Nuclear Research (CERN stands for its French name 'Conseil Européen pour la Recherche Nucléaire') in Switzerland and the other at Brookhaven National Laboratory, New York. So we came to know that antiprotons and antineutrons do combine to form antinuclei.

In 1995, a CERN team led by German physicist Walter Oelert created antihydrogen atoms for the first time. Nine of these atoms were produced during collisions between antiprotons and atoms of the rare gas xenon, which, took place over a period of three weeks. Each atom had a lifespan of about 40 billionth of a second. Each travelled at a speed close to that of light over a distance of 10 metres, collided with ordinary matter, and was destroyed.

This was the first time that antimatter particles had actually been brought together to create complete atoms. Detailed measurements of antihydrogen could now be made. By comparing hydrogen and antihydrogen atoms, scientists would now be able to understand the differences between matter and antimatter.

## How Can the Universe Exist?

If theory is to be believed, the Big Bang should have created equal amounts of matter and antimatter. But whenever matter and antimatter come into contact, they destroy each other, leaving only energy behind. So shouldn't the universe have died as soon as it was born? Yet, here we are. The current explanation for this is that there was **one extra matter particle** for every billion matter–antimatter pairs.

Just one extra particle for every billion perfectly matched pairs and that is the reason that the universe did not die as soon as it was born. Physicists are still trying to figure out how that one particle could have escaped.

Antimatter is not something that exists only in a faraway galaxy. It exists close to us as well. Cosmic rays transport small amounts of antimatter to the earth. Scientists have proof that antimatter gets produced in thunderstorms. Even bananas produce antimatter, releasing one positron every 75 minutes! This happens because bananas contain a small amount of the element potassium 40. This is an isotope of potassium, which occasionally releases positrons as it decays. Potassium 40 has an atomic mass of 40, while normal potassium has 39. Even our bodies contain potassium 40, which means that we are also positron-emitters! However, all these antimatter particles get destroyed as soon as they

come into contact with matter. Their life is incredibly short.

The word that physicists use for this is 'annihilation' – total destruction. When we have matter–antimatter annihilations, huge amounts of energy are released. When a gram of antimatter is annihilated, the energy produced is of the same magnitude as that produced by a nuclear bomb.

However, we humans produce only tiny amounts of antimatter. If we were to annihilate all the antimatter we have ever produced, we would not be able to release even the small amount of energy needed to boil a cup of tea. The difficulty lies in the efficiency and cost of antimatter production and storage. Twenty-five million billion kilowatt-hours of energy would be needed to create 1 gram of antimatter and the cost would be over a million billion dollars!

Antiparticles have found some use in medicine. For example, positrons are used to produce high-resolution images of the body using an imaging technique known as Positron Emission Tomography (PET). Here, positron-emitting radioactive isotopes, like the ones found in bananas, are attached to substances such as glucose that can be used naturally by the body.

These isotopes are injected into the bloodstream,

where they break down naturally and release positrons. The positrons come into contact with electrons in the body and get annihilated, which produces gamma rays that are used for creating images. In the near future, antimatter may also come in useful in cancer therapy. Scientists at CERN are currently studying antimatter with this goal in mind.

In theory, antimatter rocket propulsion is possible, so antimatter has the potential to serve as fuel for vehicles. The only limitation is that one has to gather enough antimatter so that it can happen. We do not currently have the technology to mass-produce or collect enough antimatter for this purpose. However, if we are able to find a way to create or collect large quantities of antimatter, travel to other star systems and galaxies aided by antimatter propulsion could become a reality!

## We Know Only 5 Per Cent

For decades, physicists had agreed that the universe was expanding, but gravity, as the force that pulls all matter together, would slow down the expansion over time. Then in 1998, using the Hubble Space Telescope – at that time the world's most powerful telescope – scientists discovered that the expansion was not slowing down. In fact, it was speeding up!

No one has been able to figure out why this is happening, so scientists have thought up something called **'dark energy'** that we cannot physically spot or measure. We can calculate the amount of dark energy in the universe because we know how it affects the universe's expansion. The rest is a total mystery. Physicists believe that roughly 68 per cent of the universe is dark energy. 'Dark matter' makes up about 27 per cent. The rest – everything that we can see or sense with all our instruments – adds up to less than 5 per cent of the universe.

What is the source of this 'dark energy'? One possibility is that it is produced by space itself. That sounds odd, but space is not nothingness as most of us assume it to be. It grows by itself, and as it grows, the energy will also grow if space is producing it. Another possibility is that Einstein's theory of gravity is not correct. But no one knows what a new theory of gravity would be.

What is dark matter? First, it is dark – that is, it is not in the form of stars and planets that we can see. Second, it is not normal matter. Third, it is not antimatter, because if it were, every time it collides with matter, it would be radiating unique gamma rays. There is no sign of that. So, as of now, we have no idea what makes up almost 95 per cent of the universe!

# 20

# Smaller and Smaller Particles

John Dalton developed the atomic theory to explain matter in terms of atoms and their properties. J.J. Thomson discovered the electron and Ernest Rutherford concluded from his experiments that there was a tiny positively charged nucleus at the centre of the atom, around which electrons revolve. Rutherford also discovered protons, which live inside the nucleus. James Chadwick completed the picture of the atom by discovering the neutron. However, this was not the end of the story. There were still smaller particles to be discovered.

Till date, scientists have discovered more than 200 sub-atomic particles and everyone is sure that there are many more lurking around.

## The Four Forces

Particle physicists devote themselves to the study of physical processes that take place at the sub-atomic level. At the same time, they continue to try and answer the most intriguing questions about the universe at large. How did the universe begin? Why is mass distributed across the universe in a particular way? Why is there more matter than antimatter?'

The answers to these questions can be found by understanding how particles interact with one another. Scientists have classified all the known forces of the universe into four important categories, known as **fundamental forces**. In decreasing order of strength, these are strong nuclear force, electromagnetic force, weak nuclear force and gravitational force. These forces bind matter together. Without them, there would be no galaxies, no stars, no sun and no life.

Strong nuclear force, the strongest of the four forces, is a powerful attractive force that acts only over extremely short distances. It has a range of about $10^{-15}$ metres. This is the force that holds protons and neutrons together within atomic nuclei. Electrons are not affected by this force.

Then we have electromagnetic force, which can act over very large distances. Its range is practically

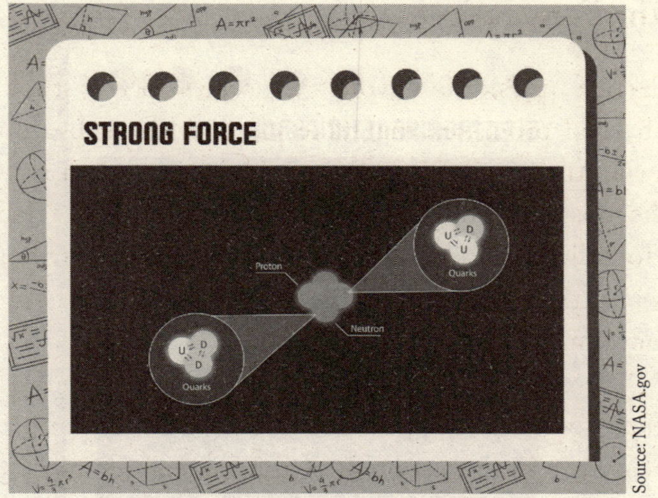


Source: NASA.gov

*The strong nuclear force binds quarks together to form protons and neutrons, and then makes sure that the protons and neutrons don't fly apart and break down the atom's nucleus.*

infinite. Charged particles interact through this force. The electromagnetic force can be attractive or repulsive depending on whether we are talking about oppositely charged particles or similarly charged particles. The magnetic force is linked to the way charged particles are moving. It was James Clerk Maxwell's genius that unified electric and magnetic forces into a single electromagnetic force. This is the force that is responsible for electrons revolving around the nucleus and for molecular bonding.

Source: NASA.gov

*Electromagnetic force binds objects with opposite electrical charges, such as the proton and electron in a hydrogen atom.*

Weak nuclear force acts over very short distances, of the order of $10^{-18}$ metre, and is many orders of magnitude weaker than the strong force. It comes into play during the decay of unstable elementary particles, particularly during beta decay, when a neutron disintegrates to produce a proton and an electron, which is thrown out of the nucleus. The weak interaction also plays a role in initiating nuclear fusion reactions that fuel the sun.

Gravitational force acts between objects having mass and can act over infinitely large distances. This is the

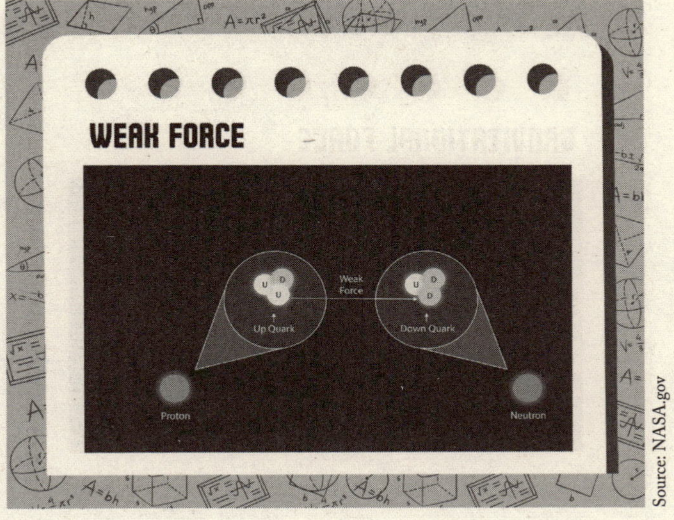


*Weak force can change an up quark to a down quark. That change can turn a proton into a neutron, or vice versa.*

force that keeps us on earth and is responsible for the motion of the planets around the sun. Gravity is the weakest of the four forces.

If you took the strength of the strong nuclear force as 1, the relative strength of the electromagnetic force would be 1/100, that of the weak nuclear force would be 1/100,000 and the strength of the gravitational force would be $1/10^{38}$. This is close to something you would get if you took a milligram of matter and compared its mass to that of the sun!

*Gravity can be described as the bending and curving of the fabric of space-time. Anything with mass, like the earth and moon, or even tables and chairs, makes these distortions.*

## A Crowd of Particles

When physicists discovered that there were hundreds of sub-atomic particles, they realized that a new model was needed to explain the atomic structure, taking into account all these particles.

The most accepted model for particle physics so far is called, simply, the **Standard Model**. In the Standard Model, all the matter in the universe is composed of three kinds of elementary atomic particles. Quarks are the building blocks of protons and neutrons. There are six types of quarks that have been given interesting names: up, down, charm, strange, top, bottom. These are known as different flavours. Quarks participate in all the four fundamental forces, and they interact with one another via the strong nuclear force.

But all fundamental particles in the universe fall under two classes – fermions and bosons. Fermions are what make up matter; protons, neutrons, electrons, quarks are all fermions. Bosons are the force and energy carriers. Imagine a boy kicking a football into the goal. The boy and the ball would be made up of fermions and the force that carries the ball and gets it into the goal is a boson.

Each kind of force is associated with a particular boson. The electromagnetic force is carried by photons, which are bosons. Attraction between two quarks in an atomic nucleus occurs when two quarks exchange bosons called gluons. Thus, gluons carry the strong nuclear force. W and Z bosons carry the weak nuclear force. The graviton is supposed to be the carrier of the gravitational force. But it has not been detected so far and remains a hypothetical particle.

The boson is named after the great Indian physicist **Satyendra Nath Bose**. In the early 1920s, Bose, then a young professor at Dhaka University (now in Bangladesh), wrote to Einstein about the discoveries he had made in particle physics. Einstein found Bose's theory to be correct. In fact, he was so impressed that he gave Bose primary credit for the new field of study that opened up, called **Bose-Einstein Statistics**. If any scientist ever deserved a Nobel Prize, it was Bose. He never got one, but his name is immortalized in the 'boson'. Chapter 24 tells Bose's story.

## The Hunt for the Higgs Boson

The Higgs boson was the last undetected particle of the Standard Model. Physicists knew that fermions have mass, but a photon, which is a boson, does not. All the math showed that when the universe began, no particles had any mass. They all sped around at the speed of light and no particle moving at the speed of light can have mass. Stars, planets and life could only emerge because particles gained mass. So how did these particles acquire mass?

The only explanation was that there is a particle that, when it interacts with other particles, endows them with mass. In 1964, English physicist Peter Higgs proved mathematically that such a particle must exist, and his work was backed up by independent work done by Belgian physicists François Englert and Robert Brout. But for nearly 50 years, no one could find any trace of this particle.

The search for the Higgs boson was the biggest and most expensive quest in the history of physics. While the maths seemed to be correct, the particle was so difficult to find physically that scientists began referring to it as the **'God particle'**. The origin story of how that term came about is quite funny and has nothing to do with God. Nobel Prize winning physicist Leon Lederman had jokingly referred to the Higgs boson as the 'goddamn particle' because scientists had spent decades to trying to detect it and failed. People shortened it to 'God particle', and the nickname stuck.

CERN had spent years looking for the Higgs boson. In 2012, the research team finally confirmed that, using its Large Hadron Collider, it had found that the Higgs boson did exist. Higgs was awarded the Nobel Prize in 2013 along with Englert for what he had proved mathematically five decades ago.

The Large Hadron Collider was built for the purpose of solving this problem as well as for answering other unresolved questions in particle physics. The collider accelerates two sets of particles moving in opposite directions to almost the speed of light and then they are made to collide with each other. Each collision produces many new particles, which are then detected. The chance of a Higgs boson appearing and being detected is one in 10 billion. So the collider needs to smash together trillions of particles. Since the math showed that the Higgs boson is huge compared to the other fundamental particles, it would need a massive amount of energy to create. Then extremely powerful computers would go through the vast amount of data these collisions generate to locate the God particle.

The Large Hadron Collider took a decade to build and cost US$8 billion. It is the world's largest and most powerful particle accelerator and is 27 kilometres long, with a ring of magnets that are kept chilled at 271.3°C, a temperature colder than outer space and just above Absolute Zero. The discovery of the Higgs boson was seen as the final confirmation of the Standard Model.

**Ghosts in the Hadron**

The Large Hadron Collider, which winds across the border of France and Switzerland, is the world's most powerful atom smasher ever. It is used by scientists to discover and study the behaviour of sub-atomic particles.

In 2012, it found the Higgs boson and solved one of the great mysteries of physics. But since then, it has also pointed at new mysteries that we are far from solving. A few years ago, it discovered 'X' particles, so named because their structures are still unknown. These particles existed for one hundred billionth of a second after the Big Bang! The Big Bang was a superheated trillion-degree soup teeming with quarks and gluons, elementary particles that cooled and combined into the more stable protons and neutrons.

Just before this rapid cooling, some gluons and quarks collided, sticking together to form X particles that lived only for a time that we cannot even begin to imagine. But if we find out the nature of these X particles, we will be closer to knowing how our universe came into being.

Other findings by scientists working with the Large Hadron Collider raise doubts about the Standard Model. For example, a few types of quark have been observed that do not behave the way they are supposed to according to the Standard Model laws. It is possible that one day the Standard Model will be replaced by another deeper theory.

# 21

# The Power of the Atom

The discovery of the power that an atom holds within itself has changed the course of human history.

In August 1945, the United States dropped two nuclear bombs – atom bombs – on the Japanese cities of Hiroshima and Nagasaki. We do not really have an accurate estimate of the number of people these bombs killed. At least 100,000 people died instantly, and we have no idea how many died over the years from radiation poisoning. That is the power of the atom.

When chemical reactions take place, the substance undergoes a change at the atomic level and energy is often released in the form of heat. In nuclear reactions, the nucleus of the atom undergoes a change, there is a tiny amount of mass lost, and a tremendous amount of energy is released in accordance with Einstein's equation $E = MC^2$. Here E denotes the energy released, M is the amount of mass that is lost, and C is the speed of light in a vacuum.

The fission of 1 gram of uranium or plutonium in a day generates about 1 MW of power. This is the energy equivalent of three tonnes of coal, or more than 2,200 litres of fuel oil!

## The Rise of the Nuclear

The science that governs nuclear reactions was developed between 1895 and 1945, most of the developments unfolding over the last six years of that period. It was during those six years that the Second World War took place. That is the reason why most of the efforts of nuclear physicists at that time was focused on building the atom bomb. After the war ended, the attention of these scientists was diverted to the utilization of this energy in a controlled manner for powering ships and generating electricity. Since the 1950s, the focus has been on the growth and evolution of reliable nuclear power plants.

Nuclear fission was first achieved by a team led by the German chemist Otto Hahn in 1938. Hahn and his colleague Fritz Strassmann discovered that uranium atoms could be split if one bombarded them with neutrons. A little baffled by this discovery, Hahn got in touch with Lise Meitner, who was a former colleague and a physicist. Meitner, a German Jew, had fled to Sweden to escape Nazi persecution and was now living there.

Meitner was on a Christmas vacation with her nephew, the physicist Otto Frisch. Studying Hahn's letter, they made a startling discovery that would revolutionize nuclear physics and lead to the atom bomb. They realized that something previously thought impossible was actually happening; a uranium nucleus had split in two. Hahn had carried out a chemical analysis; Meitner, the physicist, explained the nuclear processes involved. She thought up the word '**fission**' for this process. That word lies at the heart of all nuclear energy research today.

## The Chain Reaction

A nuclear chain reaction occurs when the products of a single nuclear reaction cause further reactions leading to a chain of reactions that goes on and on, becoming stronger at every step. The nuclear chain reaction can release several million times more energy per reaction than any chemical reaction.

The Hungarian-born American scientist Leo Szilard was the first person to think of the concept of a nuclear chain reaction in 1933. In 1936, he tried to create a chain reaction using beryllium and indium, but was not successful. A few months after the first nuclear fission was achieved by Hahn in 1939, Frederic Joliot Curie and his team discovered neutron multiplication in uranium, which proved that a nuclear chain reaction was indeed possible.

Szilard understood the implications of this discovery. He wrote a letter to American President Franklin D. Roosevelt, warning him that it was highly possible that Nazi Germany might attempt to build an atom bomb.

The Second World War had already begun, though the US was not a part of it yet. But Roosevelt formed an advisory committee on uranium. This was in response to reports by the US intelligence agencies that German scientists were already working on a nuclear weapon. Based on the findings of the advisory committee, the US government started funding the research led by the Italian-born scientist Enrico Fermi and Szilard. Their research was focused on uranium enrichment and nuclear chain reactions.

## The Manhattan Project

On 7 December 1941, the Japanese attacked the American naval base at Pearl Harbour and the US entered the Second World War.

Within weeks of the Pearl Harbour attack, Roosevelt launched the Manhattan Project. This was the code name for the effort to develop a nuclear weapon. Most of the work was carried out in the middle of a desert at Los Alamos, New Mexico, and not the borough of New York City that it was codenamed after. Los Alamos Laboratory was secretly built and formally established on New Year's Day, January 1943. This was the complex where the first nuclear bombs were built.

The Manhattan Project gathered together **the finest scientific minds** in America, though they were from many different origins. Leo Szilard and Edward Teller were Hungarian, Enrico Fermi and Emilio Segre were Italian, Hans Bethe was German, Niels Bohr was Danish, James Chadwick and Owen Chamberlain were British. Thirty-one of the scientists involved in the project had won the Nobel Prize or would go on to win it. J. Robert Oppenheimer, a brilliant American theoretical physicist, was in charge.

On 16 July 1945, the first atomic bomb was

successfully detonated in the New Mexico desert. This was known as the 'Trinity Test'. The detonation created a 40,000-feet-high mushroom cloud and the Atomic Age was ushered in.

As he watched that enormous explosion, Oppenheimer said softly to himself: 'Now, I am become Death, the destroyer of worlds.' This was a quote from the **Bhagavad Gita**, where Lord Krishna reveals himself in all his terrible glory to Arjuna.

*Operation Crossroads, a nuclear weapon test by the US military at Bikini Atoll, Micronesia, 1946*

## Little Boy, Fat Man

The bombs that the scientists at the Los Alamos laboratory had built would end the Second World War.

In May 1945, Germany surrendered to the Allied Forces led by America and Britain, but Japan refused to do so. American military leaders were convinced that the Japanese would fight on to the bitter end, which would lead to tremendous casualties on both sides. Ten days after the Trinity Test had been successfully carried out, on 26 July 1945, the US delivered a final warning. It asked Japan to surrender immediately and form a new democratic government or face complete destruction. Japan refused.

On the morning of 6 August, an American bomber plane – named Enola Gay after the mother of its pilot Colonel Paul Tibbets – dropped a bomb on Hiroshima. This uranium-based bomb, Little Boy, caused destruction on a scale that had never been witnessed before. Since there was still no surrender, another bomb, Fat Man, was dropped on Nagasaki three days later. There was no way out now. Japan surrendered and the Second World War came to an end.

## Nuclear for Peace

Although the first use of nuclear energy had been destructive, scientists were optimistic about the future of nuclear power. They believed that nuclear reactions could be a source of affordable and endless energy. Generation of electricity by a nuclear reactor took place for the first time at the EBR-I Experimental Station near Arco, Idaho, in the US on 20 December 1951. It began by powering four 200-watt lightbulbs, and in 1955, generated enough electricity to power the small town of Arco.

In 1953, American president Dwight Eisenhower gave his famous 'Atoms for Peace' speech at the United Nations, which laid emphasis on the need to develop uses of nuclear power that would be good for the world.

In 1954, the Obninsk reactor in the Soviet Union became the first commercial nuclear power plant, supplying electricity to homes and offices. In 1974, France launched a huge nuclear power programme due to sharply rising petrol prices. Today, about 70 per cent of France's electricity comes from nuclear power.

## But the Bombs Got Bigger

For all the talk about using nuclear energy for peaceful purposes, bombs have only been getting more and more powerful. The **hydrogen bomb** or thermonuclear bomb was developed by American scientists and its first full-scale test took place in November 1952, less than six and a half years after the bombing of Hiroshima and Nagasaki.

The Hungarian-born American physicist Edward Teller had been deeply interested in developing the hydrogen bomb for many years. Even while working in the Manhattan Project, he spent most of his time trying to figure out how to design the hydrogen bomb rather than the atomic bomb. But after the Second World War ended, the US government lost interest in building the 'Super', as it was called then.

Things changed the day the Soviet Union tested its first atomic bomb in August 1949. The world now had two rival superpowers, the US and the Soviet Union, and both had the bomb. Oppenheimer very strongly opposed the development of the hydrogen bomb. He felt that the bomb would pose 'extreme danger to mankind'. But in January 1950, American president Harry S. Truman gave the go-ahead, and Teller, who

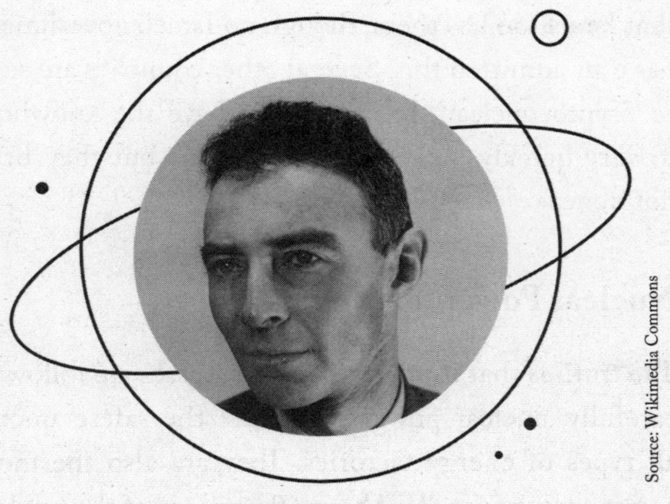


*J. Robert Oppenheimer*

hated the Soviet Union from the bottom of his heart, was put in charge. Within three years, he and his team had succeeded.

Teller's bomb, smaller in size and lighter than the ones that had destroyed Hiroshima and Nagasaki, was over 450 times more powerful than those. But less than ten years later, the Soviet Union had built a bomb that was eight and a half times more destructive than Teller's first one.

Today, eight countries officially have hydrogen or thermonuclear bombs – the US, Russia, Britain, France, China, North Korea, India and Pakistan. It is believed that Israel too has them, though no Israeli government has ever admitted this. Several other countries are seen as 'crypto-nuclear', meaning they have the knowhow to very quickly make nuclear weapons but they have not done so.

## Nuclear Power for Homes

The truth is that if proper safety processes are followed carefully, nuclear power plants are the safest among all types of energy factories. They are also the most environment friendly. About 60 per cent of the world's electricity is generated from coal, oil and gas. These fuels damage the environment. Some scientists claim that nuclear energy is **cleaner and greener** than even wind or solar power. In the long run, nuclear electricity can also be the cheapest.

But there need to be very strong safety processes because if radioactive substances leak into our air, water or earth, that could be terrible for the environment and all forms of life. There have been three big nuclear plant accidents that we know of. In 1979, a reactor at the Three Mile Island plant in America overheated, but disaster was avoided just in time. In 1986, a reactor at the Chernobyl plant in the Soviet Union, now in

Ukraine, blew up. In 2011, the Daiichi power plant at Fukushima in Japan was hit by both an earthquake and a giant tidal wave at the same time. This cut off its power supply. The reactors could not be cooled down in time and radioactive gases were released into the surrounding area.

The Chernobyl incident fuelled a global anti-nuclear movement. Today, in the Western world, only a few countries like France continue to build nuclear power plants.

It was only in the early 2000s that there was a revival of interest in this field and talk of a 'nuclear renaissance'. These talks arose out of the need to meet the world's energy crisis and the challenge of climate change.

But there is a lot of opposition to nuclear energy because most people, when they hear the term, immediately think of Hiroshima and Nagasaki. In fact, countries like Germany have shut down all their plants.

## India As a Nuclear Power

Under Prime Minister Jawaharlal Nehru, the brilliant scientist Homi Bhabha laid the foundation of a big nuclear science programme in 1948, just a year after Independence. Prime Minister Indira Gandhi conducted a peaceful nuclear explosion test in May 1974. In May 1998, under Prime Minister Atal Behari Vajpayee, India carried out a series of thermonuclear bomb tests deep under the Thar Desert in Rajasthan. A day after the tests ended successfully, India declared itself to be a nuclear weapons state.

Today, nuclear power is the fifth-largest source of electricity in India. The government has said that it intends to set up many more nuclear plants.

**India's Nuclear Man**

*Homi Bhabha*

Homi Jehangir Bhabha (1909–1966) is known as the 'father of the Indian nuclear programme'. Born into a rich aristocratic family, he went to study engineering at Cambridge University. But once there, he became fascinated with theoretical physics and mathematics.

His father gave him permission to pursue theoretical physics, but only if he passed his engineering exams with a first class. Bhabha did that.

Because of his association with the nuclear programme, few Indians know of his contributions to theoretical physics. Bhabha Scattering explains how electrons and positrons would behave if they collide. The Bhabha-Heitler Theory is on the production of electron and positron showers in cosmic rays. It was he who suggested the name 'meson' for a certain type of particle and that is what they are known as today. He was the first person to calculate the electron-proton creation and destruction process using Dirac's theory, which we discussed in Chapter 19. You can see that he was always deeply interested in what goes on inside an atom. He was one of many Indian scientists who deserved a Nobel Prize but never got it.

Bhabha was in India on holiday when the Second World War broke out in 1939. Because of the turmoil in Europe, he stayed on. The rest is history.

He was far-sighted enough to realize that the development of nuclear energy would be crucial for our country's industrial growth. When Prime Minister Jawaharlal Nehru decided to start India's nuclear programme in 1948, he chose Bhabha. The Atomic Energy Commission was set up and Bhabha was its first chairman.

While Nehru fully supported him on nuclear research, the two differed on the matter of nuclear weapons. Bhabha promoted the idea of nuclear weapons for our country's defence, but Nehru didn't agree. India became a nuclear weapon state in 1998, several decades after Bhabha's proposal.

Bhabha also pushed thorium as a nuclear fuel instead of uranium because India has vast reserves of thorium whereas our uranium reserves are meagre. It is only now that India is acting on this.

He died in a plane crash in the Alps Mountains of Europe on 24 January 1966. Many people believe that he was **killed** by a foreign country to make sure that India's nuclear programme did not take off. But it did, and his legacy lives on.

# 22

# What Light Can Do for Us

In the chapter titled 'The Story of Light', we talked about how the understanding of what light is developed over the ages. We also discussed how this knowledge helped in the invention of early optical instruments such as lenses, the telescope and the microscope.

In 1960, there was a huge breakthrough in the field of optics. The **laser** was invented. This opened the doors to many other inventions related to light. As a result, optical technology is now one of the fastest growing technologies in the world. Inventions in this field have touched various areas of our lives.

The invention of the laser fired the imagination of writers as well as scientists. In the 1964 film *Goldfinger*, secret agent James Bond was almost chopped in half by a powerful laser beam by the villain! In the *Star Wars* universe, we have laser swords called 'lightsabers'.

Today, lasers have a wide variety of applications. DVD players, supermarket scanners, optical communication and optical data storage are some of the areas where lasers are applied.

## What Is a Laser?

The word stands for 'light amplification by stimulated emission of radiation'. It is a very narrow beam of light with atoms that have a very small range of wavelength. In physics terms, it is 'a highly directional beam of monochromatic and coherent light'.

'Highly directional' means that the beam is sharply focused on a target. 'Monochromatic' means 'one colour'. And the word 'coherent' means that light waves are in the same phase or in sync with each other. Waves in the same phase add up to give a far bigger wave, so light waves add up to give a powerful beam.

It was Einstein who gave us the principle of the laser in 1917. We know that electrons in a material move in orbits. An electron can absorb energy from an electrical current or light and move from a lower energy orbit to a higher energy orbit. When the electron returns to its lower energy orbit, it radiates energy in the form of a photon. This is known as **spontaneous emission.**

If we use an energy source to pump up the energy of the material, we can have something known as 'population inversion'. This means that there are now more electrons in the higher energy level than at the lower level. When all these electrons come down together to the ground state, they emit a beam of monochromatic light. This is of course a simplified explanation. The actual physics is far more complicated.

## A Long History

Although Einstein gave us the principle of the laser in 1917, it took physicists more than 40 years to come up with a working model. An in-between step was the invention of a working 'maser' – microwave amplification of stimulated emission of radiation – by American physicist Charles H. Townes and his colleagues in 1953. The maser is now used for satellite communication. Townes and Arthur Leonard Schawlow worked together, took the idea of the maser forward, and designed the first laser.

Schawlow presented the idea of having a set of mirrors inside the device's cavity to bounce the light back and forth in a particular direction so that the beam of light would be unidirectional. The dimensions of the device would be adjusted to have only one frequency of light. They patented the idea in 1958. The first laser was built by Theodore H. Maiman at Hughes Research Laboratories based on this design.

But Gordon Gould, another American physicist, had also independently designed the laser and built a working model. He carried out and won a 30-year fight with the United States Patent and Trademark Office to obtain patents for laser and related technologies.

With lasers came the possibility of communication using light waves. Electromagnetic waves had been used earlier for this purpose. Radio waves were employed in television and radio. Microwaves were used for satellite communication. Since light waves have a much higher frequency, they have a much larger information-carrying capacity. But the trouble with light waves is that they get scattered by air molecules and dust particles. This problem was solved with the development of fibre optic communication systems.

## Talking through Light

Optical fibres are made of glass or plastic. They are approximately as thick as a human hair, cylindrical, and consist of a core that has a slightly higher refractive index than the outer layer known as the 'cladding'.

When a ray of light passes from one medium into another, it may bend. The refractive index of a medium measures how much it can bend a ray of light. If the refractive index is high, and the ray hits the interface of the two mediums at a certain angle or higher, total internal reflection occurs and the ray stays within the medium with the higher refractive index.

In an optic fibre cable, total internal reflection takes place at the core-cladding interface, which means that there is no transmission, only reflection. As a result, light travels through the optical fibre without any loss of energy.

When bundled together, these fibres form a fibre-optic cable. Fibre-optic cables are used to link telephones and computers. We have fibre-optic cables laid on the ocean floor that connect countries across the world. They can carry a huge amount of information from one point to another extremely fast. Doctors also use fibre-optic instruments to examine the insides of the human body.

A fibre-optic communication system consists of a light source, a transmitter, fibre-optic cables and an optical receiver. The light source is usually a laser due to the simple reason that lasers emit monochromatic light. The transmitter converts an electrical digital signal into a light signal. The signal is then superimposed on laser light as variations of intensity and pulse rate.

If the light beam has to travel a long distance, it is made to pass through an optical regenerator. This useful device gives a boost to the power of the ray by copying the message and sending the duplicate forward to its destination. It's like a relay race. When the beam of light arrives at the optical receiver, it is decoded and the original signal retrieved.

Because of fibre optic communication systems, it is now possible to send a tremendous amount of information across thousands of kilometres, without the message getting corrupted on the way. That is, chances are extremely low that when you receive an email from a friend, you find that you can read only the first few lines and the rest of it goes '@#%@$^&*#%' and so on.

## Three New Fields

With the invention of the laser and the introduction of fibre optics, three new fields of study opened up. These were optoelectronics, electro-optics and photonics. Optoelectronics deals with the development of devices that respond to optical power, emit or modify light beams, or utilize light for their internal operation. Electro-optics is the use of electric fields to generate and control light. Photonics has the broadest definition. It is the science of generating and harnessing light.

These new fields of study have provided us with new technologies. Optoelectronic devices include the information displays that we see all around us, from our digital alarm clocks to scoreboards in cricket stadiums, remote sensing systems that are used to predict the weather or map remote parts of our planet without actually going there, and solar cells which convert light energy into electricity. Smart phones and smart watches use electro-optical sensors that convert light to energy.

When we wake up in the morning, light helps us see the world around us. But light is also, in a way, one of the most important factors in our understanding of the universe. All modern physics, from how and why subatomic particles behave as they do to building bombs that can destroy all life on earth, is built on the basic fact that the speed of light is constant everywhere and at all times. **It never changes**, no matter what happens. That's really quite a glorious thing to think about.

## The Scientist-Businessman

Source: saldef.org via Wikipedia

*Narinder Singh Kapany*

Narinder Singh Kapany is a name that very few people remember today. But Kapany (1926–2020), an Indian-American physicist, was one of the people who created the field of fibre optics. In fact, it was he who coined the term 'fibre optics' in 1960. He also wrote the first book on it. In 1999, the American business magazine *Fortune* named him one of seven 'Unsung Heroes of the 20th Century'. He was also on *Time* magazine's list of top ten scientists of the twentieth century.

While working on his PhD at Imperial College, London, under the British physicist Harold Hopkins, he developed a technique that was better than all previous techniques for transmitting images through optical fibres. Almost at the same time, the Dutch scientist Bram van Heel invented fibre cladding. These two developments jumpstarted the field.

Other than fibre optics communication, Kapany also made discoveries in the fields of lasers, biomedical instrumentation, solar energy and pollution monitoring.

A few years after moving to the United States, he founded his first company Optics Technology Inc. in 1960. He went on to set up two more, Kaptron Inc. and K2 Optronics. He also taught at several top American universities and owned patents for 120 inventions.

Two months after he passed away, the Government of India awarded him Padma Vibhushan, the country's second-highest civilian honour.

# 23

# Indian Physicists Who Won the Nobel Prize

Though many Indian scientists have deserved the Nobel Prize for physics, only two have been awarded so far. Here we tell the stories of the two who did. In the next chapter, we will talk about some who should have won.

## Confident and Angry

Sir Chandrashekhar Venkata Raman (1888–1970), or C.V. Raman, as he is popularly known, is remembered chiefly for his discovery of the Raman Effect, or Raman Scattering, which won him the Nobel Prize in 1930. India celebrates National Science Day on 28 February, the day Raman made his great discovery.

The Raman Effect is the change in the wavelength of light that takes place when a light beam is deflected by molecules. When a beam of light falls on a transparent, dust-free chemical compound, it gets scattered in different directions. The wavelength remains unchanged for most of the scattered light. However, for a small portion of the beam, there is a change in wavelength. CV Raman explained why this happens.

The **Raman Effect** can be more easily understood if we consider the particle nature of a light beam. When photons strike the molecules of the transparent material, most of the collisions are elastic, which means that they do not lose any kinetic energy or momentum. The photons get scattered with no change in energy or wavelength. But in some cases, there is an energy exchange between the molecules of the material and the photons. When this happens, the scattered light has diminished or increased energy, and so a longer or shorter wavelength.

In 1871, Cambridge University professor Lord Rayleigh, who was a lifelong mentor to the great Indian scientist Jagadish Chandra Bose, had explained that the sky is blue because of the collision of particles and their scattering. But photons would be discovered many years later. The Raman Effect explained much more precisely why the sky is blue and why it turns red at sunrise and sunset.

Raman was a child prodigy. He finished school at the age of 13. He was a scholarship student and received a gold medal in physics from the University of Madras, where he did his graduation and post-graduation. His first research paper, on diffraction of light, was published in 1906 while he was still a student. The idea of the Raman Effect came to him in 1921 when he was on his way to Europe. The wonderful blue colour of the Mediterranean Sea inspired him to ponder deeply and come up with the concept.

His work created a whole new technique in physics called Raman Spectroscopy. Today, Raman Spectroscopy is done with X-rays and laser beams by physicists and chemists to study molecules and get more information about the atomic structure of various materials.

An interesting fact about the Raman Effect is that Russian scientists Grigory Landsberg and Leonid Mandelstam discovered the exact same phenomenon on 21 February 1928, seven days before Raman. But the Indian scientist's findings were published in a scientific journal five weeks before the Russians', and so it came to be known as the Raman Effect and Raman won the Nobel Prize. Obviously, the Russians were not pleased. Even today, in Russian scientific literature and textbooks, Raman is never mentioned. They refer to Raman Scattering as 'combinational scattering of light'. From Archimedes to Newton to Raman, luck and chance have had an important role in who ends up at the forefront of the history of science.

Raman's career path was interesting. In 1907, after completing his MSc, he sat for the entrance test for the Indian Finance Service and topped it. He was posted in Calcutta as Assistant Accountant General and came into contact with the Indian Association for the Cultivation of Science, the first research institute established by Indians. With the support of the association's members and Sir Ashutosh Mukherjee, vice-chancellor of Calcutta University, he managed to get permission to do research on his own time and at any time of day or night.

Two years later, he was transferred to Burma (now Myanmar). When he returned to Calcutta as Accountant General in 1911, he continued his research. In 1914, he was chosen by Calcutta University to become its Palit Professor of Physics, named after Sir Taraknath Palit, a wealthy lawyer who had donated money to the university to set up this position. The post had been offered first to Jagadish Chandra Bose, who had declined.

It was a tough choice for Raman. If he took up the offer, his salary would be half of what he earned in the Indian Finance Service. But his passion was science. So he laid down a condition: he would not teach any classes and would be free to spend his time researching and guiding research scholars. The university agreed.

In 1926, Raman established the *Indian Journal of Physics*. This was where he published his paper 'A New Radiation' in 1928, reporting the discovery of the Raman Effect.

In 1933, he became the first Indian director of the Indian Institute of Science in Bangalore.

Raman was obsessed with winning the Nobel Prize. In 1924, he was elected a fellow of the world's most prestigious group of scientists, the Royal Society. At a function organized by Calcutta University to congratulate him, he said: 'I'm not flattered by this fellowship. This is a small achievement. If there is anything that I aspire for, it is the Nobel Prize. You will find that I get that in five years.' It took him a year more. But he was so confident of winning the prize in 1930 that he booked ship tickets for himself and his wife months before the prize winner would be announced so that he could be in Stockholm in time to receive the award in person.

Raman's life was filled with **controversies**. In 1933, he invited the great German scientist Max Born to come and spend six months at the Indian Institute of Science. Born had been forced to leave Nazi Germany and was then living in England. Born came, but Raman immediately began having problems with him.

Born had been working for many years in a field called Lattice Dynamics, the study of how atoms vibrate inside a crystal. But when he presented his theory in one of his lectures at the institute, Raman turned nasty. He had developed a different theory and claimed that Born was wrong. Most physicists across the world supported Born and thought that Raman's theory was not even very relevant.

Raman took this personally. He was rude to Born and refused to publish any article that supported Born's theory in the institute's scientific journal, of which he was editor. The German scientist liked India and was willing to take a permanent post, but Raman did not want him around. Born left after six months, and many years later, he said that he felt that Raman probably thought of him as an 'enemy'.

Born won the Nobel Prize in 1954, and in its

statement, the Nobel Committee almost admitted that it had been late in acknowledging his work. He had been nominated six times before by many scientists including Nobel laureates like Niels Bohr and Enrico Fermi.

As director of the Indian Institute of Science, Raman kept getting into trouble because of complaints about his behaviour and use of funds. He allocated most of the money to physics and neglected the other sciences. In 1936, the institute's board set up a committee to look into his conduct. The committee gave Raman two options: he could resign and leave or he could step down as director and stay on as a professor. Raman chose the second option and worked as a professor till his retirement in 1948.

Raman also hated Jawaharlal Nehru and his policies on science. According to his biographer, Uma Parameswaran, he once smashed a bust of Nehru on the floor. In 1954, he was awarded the Bharat Ratna, India's highest civilian award. But because it had been given to him by the Nehru government, he broke his medallion to pieces with a hammer. He even **publicly ridiculed** India's first prime minister a few times.

He hated the institutions that the Nehru government had created for scientific research and made offensive

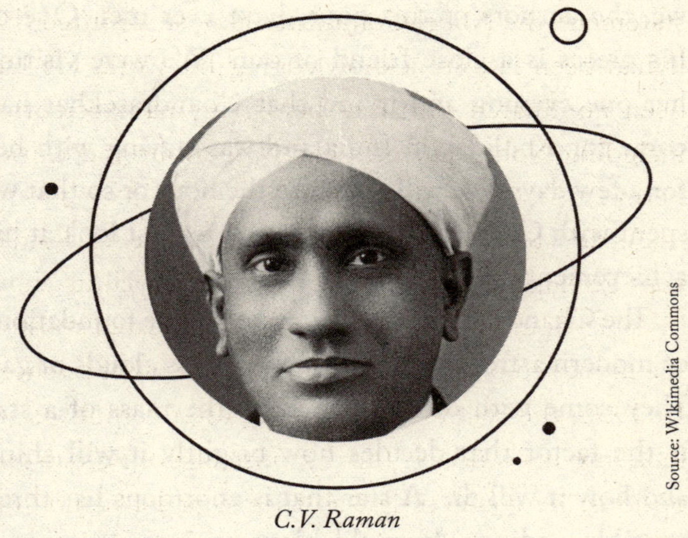

Source: Wikimedia Commons

*C.V. Raman*

remarks about the scientists, such as Homi Bhabha, who helped set them up. Once, when asked about the shortage in food production in India, he said: 'We must stop breeding like pigs and the matter will solve itself.'

He was a brilliant scientist, but he may not have been a very nice man to know!

## The Man Who Watched Stars Die

Subrahmanyan Chandrasekhar (1910–1995), who won the Nobel Prize in 1983, is the only Nobel laureate we, the authors of this book, have ever met. One of his nieces is a close friend of ours. We were visiting her one evening and found that Chandrasekhar had come for a holiday in India and was staying with her for a few days. We will return to the hour or so that we spent with Chandrasekhar later. Let us first look at his achievements.

The Chandrashekhar Limit is one of the foundations of modern astrophysics. All stars start as clouds of gas. They come with different masses. The mass of a star is the factor that decides how brightly it will shine and how it will die. A star that is enormous has three possible endings. It could blow up in a supernova, become a neutron star or a **black hole**, or end up as a white dwarf. A neutron star is a dead star whose core has collapsed, crushing all the electrons and protons together to form neutrons. A black hole is an area of such immense gravity that nothing, not even light, can escape it. A white dwarf is a small but very dense star. Its mass may be as much as the sun's, but its size or volume can be like the earth's. An average-sized star, like our sun, ends its life as a white dwarf.

The Chandrashekhar Limit is the greatest possible mass for a star to become a white dwarf. If the star weighs more than that limit, it collapses and becomes either a neutron star or a black hole. The value of this limit is 1.4 times the mass of the sun. The Chandrashekhar Limit is important because it is key to our understanding of the evolution of stars and an important factor that decides the fate of a star.

Chandrashekhar was born in 1910 in Lahore, which was part of British India at that time. As a young boy, he was taught at home by his parents and private tutors. Even as a child Chandrasekhar had an extraordinary grasp of physics. At the age of 14, he began studying for a physics degree at the Presidency College in Chennai. He wrote his first academic paper at the age of 18.

He received a scholarship to study for a PhD degree at Cambridge University. He had been informed that physicist and astronomer Ralph Fowler would be his supervisor there. On the ship from India to Britain, Chandrasekhar studied the work done by Fowler and others on white dwarf stars. He introduced the concept of relativity to the work. In fact, right there on the ship, even before he had reached Cambridge, he had done a lot of the necessary math and had discovered what would be known as the Chandrasekhar Limit. Forty-four years later, he would win the Nobel Prize for the work that he began on his first sea voyage.

It is interesting that both of India's physics Nobel

laureates got the ideas that would earn them the award on ships travelling to Europe.

After completing his PhD, Chandrasekhar stayed on in Cambridge since he was awarded a Prize Fellowship at Trinity College for 1933 to 1937. He was only the second Indian to receive this fellowship. The genius mathematician Srinivasa Ramanujan had been the first, 16 years earlier.

During this time, he met Arthur Eddington, one of the most famous British physicists of that era and became friendly with him. Eddington had explained how bright a star can possibly shine and why, and he had introduced the idea that nuclear fusion, which turned hydrogen into helium, lay at the core of stars – a theory that would be proven only years later. He had introduced Einstein's Theory of General Relativity to the English-speaking world (Einstein had written his papers in German). He had also led an expedition to the Island of Principe off the west coast of Africa to observe and take measurements during a total solar eclipse and provided the first experimental proof that Einstein's theory was correct. He was an important man in the world of physics.

In 1935, at the Royal Astronomical Society, Chandrasekhar presented his full theory on how the size of a star determines what happens to it after it dies. But Eddington had booked a talk right after Chandrasekhar's, where he trashed his theory. He proposed a different model. Chandrasekhar was surprised and deeply upset, but he was confident that he was right. The dispute continued for years, with Eddington going around saying that Chandrasekhar was wrong and both of them publishing papers in journals comparing each other's theories. In this, the young Indian received support from physicists like Niels Bohr, but the criticism of a well-known and widely respected scientist like Eddington hurt Chandrasekhar's career and delayed the acceptance of his theory.

Eddington never agreed with Chandrasekhar and passed away in 1944. However, by this time Chandrasekhar had more or less won the argument. Yet, till his last day on earth, whenever he was asked about the dispute, he never spoke a negative word about Eddington. He insisted that he admired Eddington as a scientist and remembered him as a friend.

In 1936, Chandrasekhar accepted a teaching position at the University of Chicago, where he remained for the rest of his life, even though over the years, other universities offered him double the salary he was receiving at Chicago.

He had wanted to return to India and work there, but even after looking around for a year, he could not find a suitable job. This indicates the state of scientific research in India in those days. But perhaps it was good for physics, for, being in America, Chandrasekhar could be in close touch with the top minds in the world while having full freedom to pursue his ideas.

During the Second World War, Chandrasekhar worked on ballistics, the science of launching, flight behaviour and impact effects of projectiles, especially weapons such as bullets, unguided bombs and rockets. He published many papers. J. Robert Oppenheimer, head of the top-secret Manhattan Project that was trying to build the first nuclear bomb, was impressed and offered him a job there. But the American government took too long to give him a security clearance, and he was unable to join.

During his teaching career in Chicago, which lasted nearly 50 years, he grew to be one of the most loved and respected teachers in the university, and also one of the most feared. The famous American astrophysicist **Carl Sagan**, who had been a student of his, wrote that 'frivolous questions' from unprepared students were 'dealt with in the manner of a summary execution', while questions of merit 'were given serious attention and response'.

One of his biographers has quoted a few of his students saying that if they saw Chandrasekhar coming down a street towards them, they would quickly cross the street and get to the other side so they would not have to face his piercing gaze.

A strict teacher, Chandrasekhar was committed to getting the best out of his students. He insisted that students address him as 'Professor Chandrasekhar' until they received their PhD degree, and from that day on, they were encouraged to call him 'Chandra'. When in the 1940s, he was working at a far-off observatory run by the University of Chicago, he would drive 240 kilometres every weekend to teach a course at the university. Two of the students who took the course, Tsung Dao-Lee and Chen-Ning Yang, won the Nobel Prize in 1957, 26 years before their professor did. It is a mystery why the Nobel Committee took so long to recognize Chandrasekhar's work, when several physicists who had built on his discoveries had won the prize over the decades.

Coming back to our meeting with Chandrasekhar at his niece's. When we met him, he looked like a modern rishi, still and silent in his perfectly ironed white shirt and black trousers. His eyes were bright and calm, and they seemed to dig directly down to your soul. We immediately understood why those students used to cross the street when they saw him coming.

He told us that he had retired from teaching and was now trying to develop a mathematical explanation of what beauty is in a work of art. What makes people love and cherish some pieces of art and literature forever while the vast majority of what artists and sculptors and writers produce are not paid much attention to or are quickly forgotten? He was studying works of art and literature that were universally accepted as masterpieces and was also in touch with some of the world's greatest living artists and writers. Gathering up our courage, we told him that such a mathematical formula may not be possible for art and literature. Of course, he did not agree.

In the course of our conversation, he mentioned that as a professor, he had always believed in just two grades – pass and fail, not A+ A- B+ C+ and so on. When he read the exam answer papers of his students, he would check whether the student had understood the basic concepts of what Chandrasekhar had taught. If he thought that the student had not been able to do so, he would fail the student even if they had got the answers to three out of five questions right. Someone who had managed to also answer three questions,

*Subrahmanyan Chandrasekhar*

but Chandrasekhar sensed that they had grasped the theories and were insightful, were given a pass grade.

This was scary, but we could understand his logic as a devoted teacher and believer in the core principles of how science could progress. He wanted his students to truly learn what he was teaching and not just learn enough to answer some exam questions. Our ancient rishis had also followed the same philosophy. We kept quiet.

Chandrasekhar passed way in 1995, before he could finish his work on the underlying math of great art and literature. If he had been able to do so, it would have certainly caused much discussion and many arguments all across the world of art and science.

One last interesting fact: Both Indian Nobel laureates in physics, Chandrasekhar and C.V. Raman, were from the same family. Raman was Chandrasekhar's paternal uncle, his father's cousin.

# 24

# . . . And the Indians Who Didn't Win

This is a very different chapter from the others in this book. It is about great Indian physicists who should have won the Nobel Prize but were simply overlooked or ignored. In earlier chapters, we spoke about Homi Bhabha and Narinder Singh Kapany. Here, we tell the stories of the four men who absolutely deserved to win the highest honour in the world of physics. Most of us do not know about them or remember them today, but their stories must be told.

## The Idealist

Sir Jagadish Chandra Bose (1858–1937) was perhaps the greatest Indian scientist of modern times. His inventions lie at the heart of much of the technology we now take for granted in our everyday lives.

Though the Italian scientist Guglielmo Marconi has been traditionally credited as the inventor of the radio, the apex world body Institute of Electrical and Electronic Engineers, better known as IEEE (pronounced I Triple E), has now officially acknowledged that Bose was the father of wireless communications. It is his work, done in the late nineteenth century, that forms the foundation of technologies that power devices ranging from cell phones to microwave ovens, radios to radar, satellite television to the world's most powerful space telescopes.

And he achieved all this while facing extreme **racial discrimination** from the British Raj.

Bose demonstrated the use of radio waves in 1895 in Calcutta, two years before Marconi conducted his wireless signalling experiments. In 1896, he exhibited the devices he had invented in the Royal Institute in London to an audience that included the best scientists of Britain. They were awed by what he had done. Marconi, who was then living in London, may have been in that audience and may have even met him. In any case, British newspapers carried many articles about Bose and interviews with him, and we know that Marconi avidly followed every piece of news on wireless communication systems as he was working on developing his own.

When Marconi finally managed to send radio signals over great distances, he almost certainly used Bose's radio transmitter technology. The design was the same, except for a very minor and meaningless tweak. Marconi may have done this to hide his theft. In fact, he later admitted that he did not really understand the science behind the transmitter he claimed to have built.

British companies pleaded with Bose to not make the design of his devices public. They wanted to buy his technology and were willing to share half their profits with him. This would have made Bose enormously wealthy, but he refused. He believed that whatever he did should be for the good of mankind, and it was against his ideals to earn money from his discoveries. He refused to patent his inventions. Consequently, other scientists had free access to the workings of whatever he had invented. Marconi, who was an excellent businessman in addition to being a very good scientist, became a millionaire and was awarded the Nobel Prize. In his acceptance speech in Stockholm, he mentioned several scientists whose work he had built upon and improved. The one name he did not mention was Bose's. When

Marconi's Nobel Prize was announced, Bose's friends in India, Britain and America were angered. But Bose shrugged it all off; these awards meant nothing to him. He had done his work and was happy.

Bose's personal life, too, was fascinating. His father, Bhagawan Chandra Bose, who was the deputy magistrate of the district, sent him to a local Bengali-medium *paathshala* instead of the nearby English-medium school. He wanted little Jagadish to learn his mother tongue and Indian culture, and never be uppity about being born in a well-to-do family. Most of his classmates and friends were sons of local peasants; some of them were, in fact, sons of the servants in Jagadish's home. Many years later, Bose would say that because of the four years he spent in that *paathshala*, he had never been able to understand the distinctions between castes and religions.

When he was 12, Jagadish was admitted to the prestigious St Xavier's School and sent off to live on his own in Calcutta. After completing his graduation from Calcutta University, he thought of becoming a civil servant, but his father, who was himself a civil servant, told him that he should not serve the British as Bhagawan Chandra had been doing all his life; he should become a doctor or a professor. Jagadish went to London to study medicine and then shifted to Cambridge University to study physics, which was then called natural sciences.

In addition to being a very bright student, Jagadish was an excellent sportsman. He played cricket, began riding horses at the age of eight and hunted wild boars and tigers, though later in life, he gave up hunting and spoke against the killing of wild animals who were not threatening any human beings. In Cambridge, he became a keen oarsman and took part in boat races. He would often row out into the sea alone. Once, he was almost killed after getting caught in a storm off the coast of the Isle of Wight. Later, he would make the then-extremely difficult trek up to the Pindari Glacier in the Himalayas.

In Cambridge, where he was the first Indian to ever study natural sciences, the great scientist Lord Rayleigh, who would win the Nobel Prize in 1904 for his discovery of the rare gas argon, was impressed with Bose and took him under his wing. Rayleigh remained Bose's mentor and champion for as long as he lived. When Bose started doing his original research in Calcutta, he convinced the Royal Society to publish the young Indian's papers in their journal, the most respected in the world. Bose was the first Asian scientist to be published there. In 1896, Rayleigh arranged for Bose to be invited by the Royal Institute in London to demonstrate what he had invented.

After getting his degree from Cambridge University, Bose could have stayed back in England, but the call of the motherland was too strong. However, when he applied for a job as professor of physics in Presidency College in Calcutta, the British college authorities could not believe that an Indian could be a physicist. They reluctantly gave him a job, but offered a much lower salary compared to what was given to British professors with the same or even lesser qualifications. To make it worse, they only gave him only a temporary position, not a permanent one.

In protest, Bose refused to take any salary. The British were not amused. They increased his workload to six hours of teaching every day for six days a week. This would break him, they thought; he would resign and run away. But Bose took on this injustice calmly. He rose to the challenge and performed all his duties efficiently. This was the first time that a peaceful and determined mode of protest was carried out in India – what would be called ***'satyagraha'*** many years later by Mahatma Gandhi.

Soon, it became obvious to everyone that Bose was

the best and most popular science professor in the college. Students almost fought among themselves to be seated in the first rows in his classrooms. Finally, after he'd worked two years without a salary, the British authorities were embarrassed enough to make amends. They made him a permanent employee and paid him all that they owed him, though he would still be earning less than the British professors.

However, when Bose wanted to have his own laboratory to study electromagnetic waves, the bosses put their foot down once again. Sure, he was a good teacher, but how could an Indian ever do original

Source: Wikimedia Commons

*J.C. Bose*

research? They gave him a 24-square-foot space – 6 feet by 4 feet – next to a toilet and told him that he would have to pay out of his own pocket for whatever research he wanted to do.

This did not deter Bose. He designed his own equipment and got it built with the help of a semi-literate tinsmith called Nankuram, who understood nothing about what he was making. Despite this, Bose managed to get the equipment made with perfect precision. Often at night, he would sleep in his tiny laboratory under his research table, side by side with Nankuram. Eventually, he achieved what the most well-equipped and well-funded scientists in the US and Europe had failed to. All this, with everyone around trying to bring him down.

In the late 1880s, the German scientist Heinrich Hertz had experimentally proven the existence of electromagnetic waves that Maxwell's equations had predicted. He had also attempted to transmit these waves, but the equipment he had designed was huge and very expensive. Given his space and money constraints, Bose had to build a transmitter and a receiver for these waves that would be cheap to make and small enough to fit inside two suitcases. Hertz died young, in 1894. That was the year Bose began his work in his laboratory with Nankuram.

Within 18 months he had succeeded. He had discovered 'millimetre waves', now called microwaves. In 1895, in Calcutta, and next year in London, he gave a public demonstration of his work, where he used radio waves to ring a bell, **fire a gun** and blow up a heap of gunpowder that was in another room behind a very thick wall. No one in the world had ever been able to do anything like that ever. This time, the British were impressed.

When Bose kept stubbornly refusing to get any of his inventions patented, Swami Vivekananda, who was a friend and admirer, got tired of his idealism. He took the design of a device that Bose had built and asked one of his American disciples to get it patented. Finally, in 1904, Bose was awarded a patent for what was the world's first semiconductor device. He became the first Asian to be awarded a US patent. But he refused to renew the patent the next year.

Sir Nevill Mott, who won the Nobel in 1977 for his contributions to semiconductor physics, said: 'J.C. Bose was at least 60 years ahead of his time. In fact, he had anticipated the existence of p-type and n-type semiconductors.' We won't go into what those are, but let's just say that we would not have any laptops or iPads or cell phones without this technology.

Within five years of his first Royal Institute lecture, Bose abandoned electronics and shifted his focus to plant biology, attempting to prove that plants are living beings as much as we are, and feel joy, sadness and pain just as humans and animals do. He developed a highly sophisticated instrument, which he named the **'crescograph'**. This instrument could record and measure a plant's response to external stimuli and magnify their tiny movements up to 10,000 times. He had invented what we now call the science of biophysics – the use of physics to study biology.

We know today that most of his findings are true. But at the time, European botanists and physiologists, who considered Bose to be an intruder into their domains, ridiculed his research and trashed his work. Bose, as usual undaunted, stood firm and confident of his findings.

Rabindranath Tagore was Bose's closest friend. In fact, it was Bose who convinced Tagore that he should not be writing only poetry and songs and must write more prose, short stories and novels. He insisted that Tagore must write a short story every week and would have to read it out to Bose when he visited his home every weekend. Thus were born some of the finest Indian literary works, including the popular short story

'Kabuliwala' and the novel *Gora*. Interestingly, Bose, too, was a writer. He wrote the first Indian science fiction story, about a man who tames a cyclone with a bottle of hair oil.

Bose has a crater on the moon named after him – a lunar impact crater situated in the southern hemisphere of the moon. However, despite his many achievements, he is largely forgotten today and his work on wireless communication remains little known. But remember, every time we switch on our laptop or connect via wi-fi to the internet, it is the technology pioneered by this selfless man that makes it all possible.

## The Other Bose

Satyendra Nath Bose (1894–1974), a student of Jagadish Chandra Bose at Presidency College, Calcutta, was a brilliant mathematician and physicist. There are lots of funny stories about him, most of which we are sure are not true, but they give a sense of the respect that people had for his intelligence.

For instance, it is said that a teacher in Bose's school gave him 110 out of 100 marks in a paper and predicted that he would be a great mathematician one day. There is a story that Niels Bohr once got stuck with a problem during a lecture in Calcutta and Bose resolved it instantly. It is even believed that some of his students earned their PhDs based on calculations they found on scraps of paper from his wastepaper basket!

He and Meghnad Saha, another great Indian physicist whom we will talk about later in this chapter, were close friends in college but competed for the first place. One story goes – almost certainly untrue – that in the evening after an exam, both of them sat glumly by the river Hooghly. Saha said, 'I have done very poorly. There was that 30-mark question that I just could not solve.' Bose replied, 'You're sad? That was the only question I could solve, but it took me two hours, so I didn't have time to answer any other question.' Apparently, their professor was so amazed that someone had been able to work out that answer that he gave Bose higher marks than Saha.

Rabindranath Tagore dedicated his book *Vishwa Parichay*, in which he expressed his ideas on science, to Bose.

Satyendra Nath Bose is best known for his contribution to the field of quantum mechanics. Based on Bose's work, Einstein predicted a new state of matter, which was named the Bose-Einstein Condensate. At around the Absolute Zero temperature, atoms and sub-atomic particles coalesce to form a new state of matter in which thousands of atoms condense into a single giant atom that behaves like a wave. Particles that follow Bose's statistical predictions have been named bosons in his honour. Unfortunately, while most physicists know of the Higgs boson and Peter Higgs, the British scientist, very few would have any idea why a fundamental particle is called a boson.

At the other end of the cosmic scale is the supernova – the gigantic explosion when a massive star dies. The light that a single supernova emits can be equivalent to that of an entire galaxy. And a certain type of supernovas is called **bosenovas**. These are tiny supernovas that can occur in Bose-Einstein condensates when the magnetic field around them is reversed. So when the atoms repel one another, the condensate swells up, as expected. But when the atoms attract one another, something strange happens. The condensate shrinks and then suddenly explodes, throwing atoms outwards. And stranger still, half the original atoms in the condensate seem to simply vanish.

Of course, atoms can't just disappear. They have to be around in some form or the other, but till now, no one has figured out the answer. Perhaps they merge with one another to form new molecules. Or perhaps they fly away so fast that our instruments can't spot them. Whatever the reason, bosenovas remain some of the most mysterious phenomena in the universe.

Bose is the only scientist in history whose name is associated with both the smallest particles in the universe and the biggest explosions. His work spans the cosmos.

In 1924, when he was only 30, working as an assistant professor at the University of Dhaka, Bose sent a paper he had written to Einstein in Germany. This paper had been rejected by British journals. Bose wrote: 'Though a complete stranger to you, I do not feel any hesitation in making such a request. Because we are all your pupils through profiting only by your teachings through your writings. I do not know whether you still remember that somebody from Calcutta asked your permission to translate your papers on relativity in English. You acceded to the request. The book has since been published. I was the one who translated your paper on generalised relativity.'

So impressed was Einstein that he personally translated Bose's paper in German and got it published in the major scientific journal *Zeitschrift für Physik*. But it still took him a few months to realize how revolutionary the Indian scientist's thesis was. He then started working on what Bose had revealed and took it forward. A new field was born in physics.

A few years later, when they met, Einstein asked Bose if he had been aware that he had added a whole new dimension to quantum physics. Bose said no, he just studied the science, had a couple of doubts and did his own thing.

Bose was a very bright student and excelled both in high school and college. His father encouraged his abilities. Every day, before he went off to work, he would give his son mathematical problems to solve. Bose always managed to solve them before his father returned.

In 1909, Bose obtained the fifth position on the merit list of his matriculation exam. He was only 15 years old. He joined the intermediate science programme at Presidency College. He completed his BSc at the age of 19 and topped his class. Then he enrolled in the Science College in Calcutta, which had been newly founded by the legendary educator Sir Ashutosh Mukherjee, for MSc. His performance in the MSc examination set a new record amongst the students of Calcutta University.

For a modern scholar, enrolment into a PhD programme would be the next logical step. However, things were more complicated for Bose. The First World War had started in 1914. Travelling to Europe for higher studies was nearly impossible.

But things started looking up for Bose and other young Indians in Calcutta who wished to pursue a career in science when PhD programmes were introduced in Calcutta University. The university was donated a large sum of money by two wealthy men for the promotion of advanced education for Indians. Sir Ashutosh Mukherjee, vice-chancellor, started spending these funds on new professorships, research programmes and the purchase of useful academic journals. He also gave graduate students access to his own private library of mathematics and physics books. (Ashutosh Mukherjee is remembered as an educationist, freedom fighter and lawyer, but he also had post-graduate degrees in math and physics.) These books were more advanced than the ones that were then easily available. Bose and his friend Meghnad Saha were able to read the latest textbooks and research papers.

Bose started studying the theory of relativity as a research scholar at the Science College. In 1921, he joined Dhaka University's department of physics as a reader – a junior professor. In 1924, he wrote a paper on Max Planck's 'quantum radiation law'. He derived this law using an approach that was completely different from what had been done till then, without any reference to classical physics ideas. This study revealed the deeper nature of light – something even Einstein had missed.

British scientific journals rejected the paper. Perhaps many of their editors had still not understood quantum mechanics or perhaps they could not believe that a 30-year-old Indian could actually think up something new in theoretical physics. Bose boldly sent his research paper to Einstein. The two then worked together to expand on Bose's concept.

Einstein had already won his Nobel Prize by then and was very famous, but he recognized the importance of what this young man in Dhaka had done. So he put Bose's name first, before his own, and gave us the Bose-Einstein Condensate and Bose-Einstein Statistics. Einstein never gave this honour to any other scientist. In fact, no other scientist's name is associated with Einstein's discoveries.

Due to the success of his research paper, Bose got the opportunity to work for two years at European laboratories. He carried out studies in X-rays and crystallography. During this time, he collaborated with many Nobel laureates, including Madame Curie, Louis de Broglie (who had discovered the wave nature of electrons) and of course Einstein.

Bose received many awards and accolades. He was a fellow of the Royal Society. He received the Padma Vibhushan award in 1954, the highest civilian honour in India after the Bharat Ratna. C.V. Raman was awarded the Bharat Ratna the same year. In 1959, Bose was named National Professor, which is the highest position in India for a scholar. He stayed in this post for 15 years till he passed away.

Throughout his life, Bose never cared for awards and accolades, fame or fortune, just like his guru Jagadish Chandra Bose. Over the years, he was asked many times about the supposed injustice that he had not won the Nobel. He would just brush away the questions cheerfully. It did not matter to him. He was a true *sanyasi* of science who had risen above worldly matters.

A close friend of ours met Bose for a few minutes when he was eight or nine years old, and the great physicist must have been close to 80 then. He was the chief guest in an awards ceremony of a children's art competition in Calcutta where our friend had won a prize. Bose walked with the help of a stick, but our friend says he can never forget his mischievous smile and the twinkling eyes behind his thick glasses.

The boy's parents asked Bose to give some life advice to the child. The old man laughed. He patted the child

Source: Wikimedia Commons

*Satyendra Nath Bose*

on his head and told the parents: 'I was an extremely naughty boy and my parents had given up on me. Now people keep asking me to give advice to children. What can I tell them? I was the naughtiest child.' Our friend's parents were a bit disappointed.

Basically, he was the **coolest Indian scientist ever**.

## The Scientist-Politician

Meghnad Saha (1893–1956) was one of the most brilliant astrophysicists of the twentieth century. Astrophysics uses the laws of physics to understand how the universe works. The Saha Concept or the Saha Ionization Equation, which he developed in 1920 when he was only 27 years old, is one of the most important theories that modern astrophysics is based on. It relates the ionization state of a gas to its temperature and pressure, combining ideas of quantum mechanics and statistical mechanics.

Saha's equation laid the foundation for stellar spectroscopy, which is an important branch of astrophysics. In fact, it changed the direction of astrophysics. Spectroscopy is the study of spectra. A spectrum is a chart that displays the intensity of light as it is emitted over a range of wavelengths. For example, a rainbow is a spectrum which occurs naturally. A stellar spectrum can reveal many properties of stars, like their chemical composition, temperature, density, mass, distance and luminosity. Spectroscopy is used to study the physical properties of all types of celestial objects – planets, galaxies, even black holes. In fact, like his Presidency College professor Jagadish Chandra Bose and his close friend Satyendra Nath Bose, he created a whole new field of knowledge.

Saha's work was not limited to astrophysics. When he visited the US on a lecture tour some months after the nuclear bombs had been dropped on Hiroshima and

Nagasaki, his deep knowledge of how nuclear energy works scared the American government so much that he was interrogated by the Federal Bureau of Investigation (FBI) and followed around everywhere he went. How could an Indian know so much? Had somebody from the Manhattan Project been secretly passing him information? **This man could be dangerous!**

Saha did not have an easy life. Unlike the two Boses, who came from well-educated and 'socially respected' families, he was the fifth child of a village grocer who struggled to keep his family away from starvation and could not afford Meghnad's education. But his merit earned him a scholarship at a prestigious school in the city of Dhaka and a kindly doctor offered him free boarding and lodging. Saha remained deeply grateful to this gentleman, even after he had become a famous scientist.

In 1905, Viceroy Lord Curzon divided Bengal into two parts and the Swadeshi movement erupted. Meghnad, barely a teenager then, took part in the movement. As a result, he was expelled from school and his scholarship taken away. But he managed to finish his studies even with great financial hardships and got admission in Presidency College in 1913, from where he graduated with top honours in mathematics.

Saha's life outside the classroom was often miserable. He faced discrimination from other students due to his caste. At his college hostel, 'upper-caste' students objected to him eating in the same dining hall as them. But through all this, his best friend Satyendra Nath Bose stood by him.

In 1920, at the age of 27 when he was a lecturer in Calcutta University Science College and taught quantum mechanics, Saha put forth the ionization formula that explained the presence of spectral lines. This was a major breakthrough in the world of physics. When atoms are excited, they emit light of certain wavelengths that correspond to different colours. This light appears as a series of coloured lines with dark spaces in between them. Each element produces a unique set of spectral lines. By studying the line spectrum, scientists can identify elements, from traces of them on earth to the composition of stars. It was Saha's work that led to this knowledge.

After he had developed his theory, Saha spent two years in London and Berlin. He knew that his theory needed experimental confirmation, but to his dismay, he found that some senior British astrophysicists had alleged that his work was nothing original; he had just put a little spin on what scientists in Britain had already done. This was, of course, nonsense. Yet, he was denied a laboratory and equipment. It was the same sort of racism that his teacher Jagadish Chandra had faced.

Much of this was not because of genuine doubts about Saha's theory but because of his politics. Saha openly supported the Indian freedom movement, so even many Indian scientists (who were loyal to the British Raj) trashed his work and actively campaigned against him. But his theory had been quietly accepted across the world and well-funded American and European scientists were working hard to provide experimental proof for it. All that Saha, who had neither money nor research equipment, could do was watch helplessly.

Eventually, the tide began turning. Saha published more papers, taking his mathematical calculations and theories forward, though he continued to face multiple rejections. In time, some of the scientists who had sneered at him began to see the truth of how Saha was opening up the world in a new way. In 1927, at the age of 34, he was elected a fellow of the Royal Society. This enabled him to raise money and start his own laboratory in Allahabad.

Over the next few years, however, he became better known to the public for his political activism than his science. In many public speeches, he spoke about an 'indigenous, home-grown and self-sufficient' science as poverty-stricken India's saviour, and rejected Mahatma Gandhi's 'back-to-village' charkha-khadi philosophy. He believed that when Independence came, it would be a false freedom if India remained dependent on Western science and technology.

His interest had now shifted from theoretical physics to nuclear science. He believed that solving complex equations to develop abstract theories would not help India. In 1939, he convinced Jawaharlal Nehru to help him raise funds to build a cyclotron for India, a particle accelerator that a few years later would prove crucial to America building the world's first nuclear bombs. However, not enough money could be raised, and the cyclotron could not be built.

But he did manage to frighten the Americans. How could an Indian know so much?

Saha stood in the first Lok Sabha election of independent India in 1951 and was elected by a large margin. In Parliament, he was often very critical of the Nehru government in many areas, though always fair and logical. Nehru and he continued to respect each other. Explaining his logic of entering politics, he noted that scientists are often accused of living in their own world, not troubling their minds with realities. 'But science and technology are as important for administration nowadays as law and order,' he said. 'I have gradually glided into politics because I wanted to be of some use to the country in my own humble way.'

In 1952, the Government of India set up the Calendar Reform Committee headed by Saha. Different regions in the country had different calendars and almanacs, so, for instance, Diwali would be celebrated in one state on a certain day and in another state maybe three days later. This caused confusion and made governance difficult. The committee's goal was to create a revised, accurate and uniform **Indian National Calendar** to 'usher a new element of unity in India'. A national calendar would fix the dates of religious observances and standardize date documents in rural areas, which would make life for everyone much easier.

Saha's team studied more than 30 different local calendars, collected precise solar and lunar data and, in November 1955, recommended an updated version of the Saka Era calendar, which Indian astronomers had been using since the sixth century CE. On 22 March 1957, a new age began with a national calendar. This is what the Indian government follows even today, using it to decide national religious holiday dates and other purposes.

Unfortunately, Saha could not see his calendar come into effect. He passed away on 16 February 1956 from a heart attack. He had been **nominated for the Nobel Prize four times** but was always rejected.

Svein Rosseland was one of the greatest European astrophysicists of the twentieth century. He was a year younger than Saha but lived about 30 years longer. In his classic textbook *Theoretical Astrophysics*, he says: 'The impetus given to astrophysics by Saha's work can scarcely be overestimated, as nearly all later progress in this field has been influenced by it and much of the subsequent work has the character of refinements of Saha's ideas.'

The brilliant Indian astrophysicist Jayant Narlikar has written: 'Meghnad Saha's ionization equation which opened the door to stellar astrophysics was one of the top ten achievements of twentieth-century Indian science and could be considered in the Nobel Prize class.'

## The Man Who Felt Cheated

The two Boses and Saha were based in India, and maybe the West found it hard to believe that such path-breaking work could be done in Calcutta, Dhaka and Allahabad. The case of E.C.G. (George) Sudarshan (1931–2018) is different. Born in Kottayam, Kerala, he spent his entire research career in the United States, mostly as a professor at the University of Texas at Austin.

We won't go into the details of most of his work because it is extremely high-level physics. Even the names of the fields that he worked in are awe-inspiring: V-A theory, which deals with the weak nuclear force, one of the four fundamental forces that we spoke about in Chapter 20; tachyons, hypothetical particles that travel faster than light; and areas that we won't even dare to explain, like the quantum Zeno effect, open quantum systems, spin-statistics theorem, non-variance groups and density matrices.

Along with the American physicist Robert Marshak, under whom he completed his PhD at the University of Rochester, Sudarshan worked on V-A theory. On 16 September 1957, Marshak and Sudarshan submitted their paper, which had several original discoveries using V-A theory, for inclusion in a particle physics conference being held in Italy.

But unknown to them, Richard Feynman and Murray Gell-Mann, both of whom would go on to win the Nobel Prize – though not for their V-A theory work

– had been working in the same area. On the very same day, 16 September 1957, Feynman and Gell-Mann sent their paper to one of the world's leading physics journals. It was published in January 1958 and Marshak and Sudarshan's four months later. Though Marshak and Sudarshan's paper was far more mathematically sound and had a stronger theoretical basis, the world gave all the credit to Feynman and Gell-Mann.

To be fair, Feynman acknowledged that Marshak and Sudarshan's work was better and tried his best to get them the recognition they deserved. But no one seemed to listen. As late as 1985, in a letter to Marshak, Feynman wrote: 'I hope some day we can get this straightened out and give Sudarshan the credit for priority that he justly deserves . . . At any opportunity I shall try to set the record straight – as I have always done.'

In 1979, the Nobel Prize went to Steven Weinberg, Sheldon Glashow and Abdus Salam for their work on the weak nuclear force, based on Sudarshan's V-A theory. Late in his life, Sudarshan said in an interview: '(They) built on work I had done as 26-year-old student. If you give a prize for a building, shouldn't the fellow who built the first floor be given the prize before those who built the second floor?' Many years later, all the three prize winners would express their debt to Sudarshan.

Sudarshan's work on the quantum nature of light led to what is today known as the Glauber-Sudarshan Representation. Soon after developing the V-A theory, he moved to the field of optics and published a paper on mathematically representing what goes on at the quantum level inside a beam of light.

Roy J. Glauber, a physicist at Harvard University who was working on the same topic, wrote a paper criticizing the methods that Sudarshan had used. Sudarshan could not figure out what Glauber was talking about because as far as he could see, his math was absolutely accurate. Sudarshan wrote another paper to explain his ideas and sent it to Glauber before publishing it. Glauber now agreed but asked Sudarshan to include his name in the paper.

Glauber then published his own paper, in which he did not mention Sudarshan, and introduced something called 'P-representation', which was more or less just another name for Sudarshan's representation. Einstein had had the grace to give Satyendra Nath Bose's name first place in the Bose-Einstein condensate and Bose-Einstein statistics. Richard Feynman had told everyone that it was not him but Sudarshan who should get the credit. But here, the theory came to be known as Glauber-Sudarshan Representation.

In 2005, Glauber, along with two others working in the same field, was awarded the Nobel Prize. Sudarshan was ignored. Several physicists wrote to the Nobel Committee, protesting that Sudarshan should have been given the prize too and that his contribution had actually been greater. The discoveries for which the three scientists had been given the prize were all based on Sudarshan's research.

But nothing could be done now.

In 2006, the Government of India awarded Sudarshan the Padma Vibhushan.

Unlike the two Boses, Sudarshan remained angry till the end of his life for being overlooked for his achievements and spoke bitterly about what he saw as grave injustices done to him.

# 25

# The Now and the Next

The story of physics is never over. Just when people begin to think that they know everything in a certain field in science, there appears some discrepancy between theory and experiment. Or new and surprising information pops up. Scientists then have to either modify their theories or look for new explanations. And that is how knowledge evolves.

The discovery of the Higgs boson in 2012, the particle that had been mathematically predicted nearly five decades before, seemed to be the final clinching evidence that the 'Standard Model' in quantum mechanics was correct. But was it really? Since then, several previously unknown and mysterious particles have been discovered, fleeting through the universe and difficult to latch on to. And some of them seem to not be following the laws of quantum mechanics, developed with so much struggle, debate, dispute and wonder over more than a century.

Perhaps the most significant trend in physics in the last few decades is the meeting of astrophysics and quantum mechanics. Much of the information that quantum physicists work with today comes from outer space. Tremendously powerful astronomical telescopes constantly supply data on how stars and galaxies are born and die, and this gives quantum physicists new ideas about what could be going on inside an atom.

Studying the most enormous objects in the universe is helping us understand the behaviour of the tiniest particles.

And as we use more and more powerful instruments to study the cosmos and do harder and harder math, the mysteries only deepen. We keep discovering how much we don't know and how much we got wrong.

## Gravity's Waves

Gravitational waves were discovered in 2015. Einstein had predicted the existence of these waves almost exactly a century ago in 1916. According to his Theory of General Relativity, gravity occurs because massive accelerating objects like neutron stars create warps in the fabric of space-time. They create waves, or ripples, that move away from their source in all directions at the speed of light. These ripples create gravity, just as the Higgs boson creates mass.

The theory was mathematically complex and also seemed quite bizarre at that time. People did not accept it initially. Einstein himself was not too sure if the waves he was describing were really out there. However, the fact that these ripples do exist was established by Arthur Eddington when he made observations of the nature of light coming from a star during a solar eclipse in 1919.

Much work has gone into this area since then. We now know that the strongest gravitational waves are produced by gigantic events, such as black holes colliding with each other or huge stars exploding (supernovas). These waves may also be caused by neutron stars that are not perfect spheres or gravitational radiation that was born during the Big Bang.

In 1974, two American astronomers, Russell Hulse and Joseph Taylor, discovered a binary pulsar – two fast-rotating neutron stars close to each other emitting radio waves – 21,000 light years from the earth. They minutely tracked the radio emissions coming from this two-body system for four years because they knew that according to Einstein's Theory of General Relativity, this was just the sort of astronomical combination that should be radiating gravitational waves.

They concluded that the rate of radio emission when the stars got closer to each other changed exactly the way Einstein had predicted if they were radiating gravitational waves. In 1993, Hulse and Taylor received the Nobel Prize 'for the discovery of a new type of pulsar, a discovery that has opened up new possibilities for the study of gravitation'.

Here, we must understand that what Hulse and Taylor discovered proved that gravitational waves must exist. Over the next three and a half decades, astronomers kept studying pulsar radio emissions and produced further proof of the existence of gravitational waves. But these were all indirect confirmations. Where were the waves? No one could find them anywhere.

In the early 1990s, the US government began setting up LIGO, the Laser Interferometer Gravitational-wave Observatory. Laser interferometers are devices that emit powerful laser beams that merge and create an interference pattern. The merged beam allows scientists to measure everything from the smallest variations on the surface of a microscopic organism to the structure of enormous expanses of gas and dust in the far corners of the universe. LIGO's interferometers began working in August 2002.

For more than a decade, nothing happened. Then, on 14 September 2015, LIGO physically sensed the **tiniest flutter** in space-time caused by gravitational waves generated by two colliding black holes 1.3 billion light years away.

What does 'tiniest' mean here? LIGO's official website explains: 'While the processes that generate measurable gravitational waves are extremely violent, by the time the waves reach Earth they are thousands of billions of times smaller . . . much as sounds are weaker when you move further from the source. [. . . ] In fact, by the time gravitational waves from LIGO's first detection reached us, the amount of space-time wobbling they generated was 10,000 times smaller than the nucleus of an atom!'

One cannot even begin to imagine how small that is. It's a testament to the brilliant scientists and engineers who design and build instruments capable of this astonishing feat. In 2017, three LIGO scientists – Rainer Weiss, Barry C. Barish and Kip S. Thorne – were awarded the Nobel Prize.

Why was this discovery so important? Physicists

have known for a long time that there are two types of waves that are born far away in the universe and reach the earth with information about where they come from. These are electromagnetic waves (light, radio waves, X-rays and so on) and gravitational waves. So far, scientists have been using electromagnetic waves to study the universe.

If we can use gravitational waves too – we may be some decades away from that – they are going to bring us all kinds of information that we can never detect

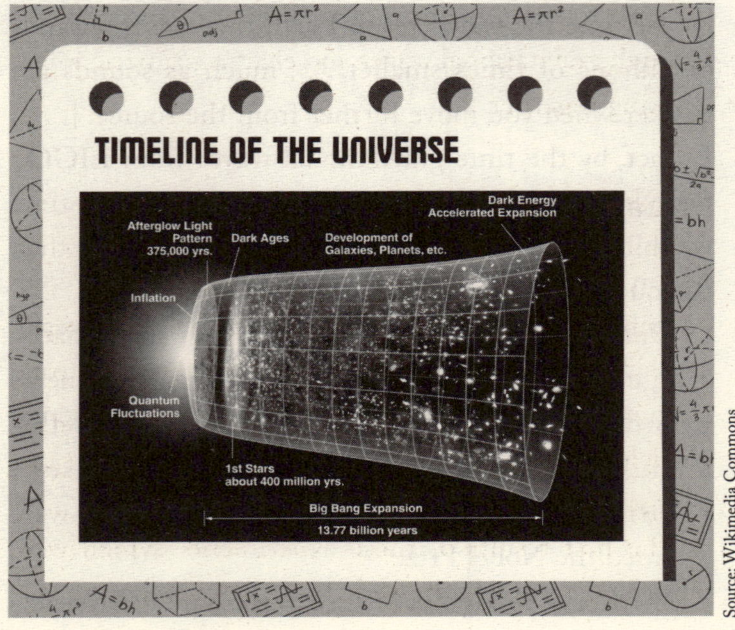


Source: Wikimedia Commons

with electromagnetic waves. For instance, gravitational waves caused by the Big Bang should still be around, undamaged and unscattered. They can tell us things about how the universe was born that we have no idea about yet.

Kip S. Thorne, one of LIGO's Nobel Prize winners, has said: 'Gravitational waves in collaboration with electromagnetic waves . . . are the foundation for the future of astronomy. Several centuries from now, when our descendants look back on this era, I think they are going to say that one of the great contributions that we gave to them is our understanding of the universe through gravitational waves and electromagnetic waves working together.'

## Strange New Particles

Muon g-2 (pronounced muon gee minus two) is an ongoing particle physics experiment that uses powerful accelerators to study how muons interact with a strong magnetic field in empty space. Muons are fundamental particles very similar to electrons. They possess the same charge and spin but are 200 times heavier.

The first results of these experiments, which were published in 2021, showed that muons behaved in a way that was not in accordance with the predictions of the Standard Model, which is the most widely accepted particle physics framework so far.

And there are other particles too which we are discovering, such as the seven **'ghost particles'** detected by the most powerful observatory on earth. Neutrinos are some of the most mysterious sub-atomic particles that we know of. They have no electrical charge, are almost without mass and move at the speed of light, don't like other particles, and rarely interact with anything. This makes detecting them very difficult. That is why they are called 'ghost particles'.

At the same time, neutrinos are also the most common particles in the universe. Approximately 100 trillion neutrinos pass completely harmlessly through our bodies every second!

You might ask – if they are not interested in us, why should we be interested in them? It is precisely because they aren't interested that we are. Since neutrinos rarely interact with normal matter, they arrive on earth in their original pure form, even though they may have travelled billions of light years. Thus, they are great messengers for phenomena happening far beyond our own galaxy. They should be able to tell us much more about our universe than all other particles that visit us from far-off places.

Deep under Antarctica lies **IceCube**, a detector that consists of more than 5,000 sensors buried inside a 1 cubic kilometre block of ice. Whenever a neutrino interacts with one of the billions of IceCube's ice molecules, the sensors record the information. By studying which sensor has detected the information and at what time, scientists can figure out which direction the neutrino came from.

They have been able to detect neutrinos with petaelectronvolts of energy, or 1,000 trillion electron-volts. In the sub-atomic world, that is huge: they carry a hundred times more energy than our atmospheric neutrinos. Obviously, they have been born out of some really enormous events that happened somewhere out there in distant galaxies a very very long time ago. IceCube scientists use neutrino data to understand fundamental high-energy processes that shape our galaxies, like exploding stars, gamma-ray bursts, and black holes and neutron stars bumping into one another.

## The Edges of the Universe

On Christmas Day in 2021, the James Webb Space Telescope (JWST), the largest and most powerful space telescope in history, set off on its journey from a launch site at Kourou in French Guiana in South America. It took 30 days to travel 1.5 million kilometres to its permanent home, a gravitationally stable spot in space called Lagrange Point 2 or L2. This allows the telescope to stay in line with the earth as our planet orbits the sun.

Using infrared, Webb is peering deep into the cosmos to uncover the history of the universe from the Big Bang onwards. One of the wonderful things about really powerful telescopes is that they take us back in time. A light year is the distance light would travel in a year, which is about 9.5 trillion kilometres. This means if we look at an object that is one light year away, we see images of what it was like a year ago. An alien studying earth from sufficiently far away would see the dinosaurs roaming around. The JWST is powerful enough to 'see' stars that are billions of light years away, which tells us what those stars were like a very long time ago. Of course, it can also see objects closer to us, so it's almost like watching a film of the universe's evolution.

From the day it settled down at L2, Webb has been sending us amazing photos of events and galaxies, the likes of which we have never seen before and are also very beautiful. They tell us how magnificent our universe is. We have also learnt a lot of new and exciting things about the cosmos and how it works.

Webb has sent back images of the four most distant galaxies known to us, which also means they are the oldest. The telescope caught the galaxies as they appeared about 13.4 billion years ago, when the universe was only 350 million years old, about 2 per cent of its current age.

Its pictures prove the existence of a **'cosmic web'** – galaxies are connected to each other through extremely long thin strings of gas and dust.

Webb has spotted the oldest black hole ever seen, a 13-billion-year-old monster with the mass of 1.6 million suns at the centre of a baby galaxy. Supermassive black holes like this anchor entire galaxies including our Milky Way. But to grow to such size, they may have also eaten up entire galaxies. We don't yet know how they became so big and at what speed. If we can find the answers to these questions, we will learn many basic truths about how the universe works and even how long it will last.

Scientists now have detailed information on the composition and atmosphere of planets hundreds of light-years away. They can study whether these planets are able to support life. Maybe one day, we will also know if there is any other planet in our universe where living creatures may exist.

Webb has let us see how stars are born. Huge

collections of dust and gas, many times larger than our solar system, slowly become increasingly dense, until suddenly hydrogen starts burning and they turn into baby stars. This will help us also know how exactly our own sun, which gives us life, came into being.

The Phantom Galaxy shines bright around 32 million light years from earth. It consists of a glowing centre with arms, which are hot dust and gas, that move in many directions and keep getting longer. Some of them become stars. Using Webb's images, scientists are confident that they will be able to figure out the areas of space where stars are formed and why. Webb has already clicked pictures of two dozen nearby star-forming galaxies.

A very interesting thing that astronomers have discovered from the Webb data is that tiny galaxies with masses less than one billion times that of our sun – yes, that's small for a galaxy – existed in the early days of the universe and may have been responsible for shaping the entire cosmos! They provided most of the light that transformed neutral hydrogen to ionized hydrogen. These were the little fellows that made the universe what it is today. But we have not yet figured out why that happened.

At the same time, the Webb Telescope has also

produced information that may disrupt much of what our physicists have been sure of about the workings of the universe. This is actually a wonderful thing, because if JWST had not thrown up some surprises, we would have learnt nothing new.

## Could We Have Misunderstood the Universe?

Nearly a hundred years ago, in 1929, the American astronomer Edwin Hubble proved that the universe is expanding like a balloon, with galaxies moving away from one another. Hubble's Law is one of the basic laws of modern astrophysics and helped scientists develop the best theory that we have so far about the birth of the universe as a result of the Big Bang.

The most powerful space telescope we had before the Webb Telescope was the Hubble Telescope. Launched in 1990, it is still working fine. Some of the data that the telescope sent back over the years puzzled scientists. It indicated that different parts of the universe are expanding at different speeds. For decades, the Hubble Constant had been accepted as the unit that describes how fast the universe is expanding at different distances from a particular point in space. Scientists have disagreed about what the true value of that rate is, but nearly everyone agreed that there is a specific rate.

So how can different parts of the universe expand at different speeds? Some astrophysicists were hoping that the much more powerful Webb Telescope would disprove this observation. But Webb confirmed that this is, in fact, true. In other words, the universe does behave like a balloon, where parts of it get bigger fast and parts of it slowly when you pump air.

This goes against all the physics that we have accepted as correct for many decades. Adam Riess, who won the Nobel Prize in 2011 for the discovery of dark energy, says that we may have misunderstood the universe. According to Riess, dark energy may be the mysterious force behind the universe's expansion, which is quickly accelerating. While it's estimated to make up 68 per cent of the universe, we know almost nothing about it.

There are various theories that are being developed to explain what is going on. Some scientists believe that the amounts of dark energy are different in different parts of the universe and control the rates of expansion. Others say that we need an entirely new physics!

For instance, there is a new theory called Modified Newtonian Dynamics that proposes that for gravitational pulls ten trillion times smaller than those felt on the earth's surface – like the pulls that distant galaxies exert on one another – Newton's laws break down, and we need new equations.

As for dark energy, it has even been theorized that the expansion of the universe may be driven by a mysterious form of matter called 'unparticles', which do not obey the Standard Model of particle physics. Dark energy, these scientists say, is made of unparticles. They claim that their theory explains the Webb Telescope's observations better than our current model of the universe does.

One Nobel laureate scientist has said that this new riddle of the cosmos is not a problem, but a 'crisis' of physics.

The more we get to know, the more we learn how little we know.

## Is the Universe Real?

The Nobel Prize in physics in 2022 was awarded jointly to Alain Aspect, John F. Clauser and Anton Zeilinger 'for experiments with entangled photons, establishing the violation of Bell inequalities and pioneering quantum information science'. This means nothing to more than 99.9 per cent of people on earth, but what the three scientists are saying based on the results of their experiments can change our entire view of what the universe is. It can even make us wonder what 'real' is.

The story begins in the 1930s when Einstein on one side, and Niels Bohr and Erwin Schrödinger on the other, got into a heated debate over how the universe operates at a fundamental level. Einstein believed that all aspects of reality – from a planet to a photon of light – must have precisely defined properties that can be discovered through measurement. That is, an apple is red even when no one is looking at it. When a tree falls in a forest, it makes a big thud, even if there is no living creature around to hear it.

But Werner Heisenberg had already proved that for sub-atomic particles, one can either know certainly where it is located or how fast it is moving, but not both at the same time. And Schrodinger had shown that a sub-atomic particle like an electron may only exist as a possibility until you go looking for it, at which point it becomes a 'real' thing.

Einstein refused to accept these theories. But Bohr and Schrödinger argued that at the quantum level, reality appeared to be fundamentally uncertain. A particle does not possess certain properties until the moment of measurement. If there were a sub-atomic apple, it is not red, and a particle 'falling tree' does not make any sound unless there is someone to see or hear them.

They also argued that all the mathematics showed that two particles that may be millions of miles away from each other can share information instantly despite having no conceivable way of communicating. Think of them as two twins, Joy and Jyoti. Joy lives in Alaska and Jyoti lives in Chennai. Joy flips a coin five times and it comes up heads, heads, tails, tails, heads. At the exact same moment, Jyoti too flips a coin and also gets heads, heads, tails, tails, heads. And this happens every time they do it.

This is unthinkable in the world that we see around us. Naturally, Einstein sneered at this theory, calling it 'spooky action at a distance', but over time, he has been shown to be wrong.

According to quantum mechanics, what binds the two particles Joy and Jyoti together is something called **quantum entanglement**. In simple terms, quantum entanglement means that aspects of one particle of an entangled pair – Joy and Jyoti – depend on aspects of the other particle, no matter how far apart they are or what lies between them. These particles could be, say, electrons, and an aspect could be the way they are spinning, in one direction or another. So when you check which way one is spinning, you know which way the other one is spinning too. And this strange connection between the two particles is instant, seemingly breaking the fundamental laws of the universe. Remember, nothing can travel faster than light. But here, the effects are instantaneous. The effect doesn't *travel*, it *appears* in two places at the exact same moment.

Einstein and others tried to explain this by proposing that there was some unknown property, which they called 'local hidden variables', that determined the state of a particle before measurement. **'Local'** means that an object can only be affected by its immediate environment and that no effect can move faster than light. But so far, no one has figured out what these hidden variables could be.

In 1964, John Stewart Bell, a brilliant Irish physicist, devised a scheme to test whether the idea of local hidden variables made sense. **'Bell's Theorem'** or 'Bell's Inequality', mentioned in the 2022 Nobel Prize citation, asserts that if certain predictions of quantum theory are correct, then our world is non-local. 'Non-local' means that an object can be affected by another object that is very far apart in space, and that effect comes sooner than any signal could have gone from one to the other, even at the speed of light.

The 2022 Nobel laureates were the first to experimentally prove that the particle world is non-local. This raises some very big questions.

Everything in our entire universe – you, me, the room that you are sitting in right now, the most gigantic galaxies – is made of particles. However, if the particles are non-local, then how real is the universe that we experience through our five senses – from the smell of a rose to the sound of a bell ringing to wonderful pictures of stars being born that our space telescopes are bringing to us? If we accept what the three Nobel laureates have proved through experiments, then the universe as we know it is not actually real. It is not a physical thing, but rather a mathematical construct.

Those of us who are familiar with the concept of Maya in the ancient Indian philosophy of Advaita Vedanta – that the world is an illusion – will not be surprised by the questions these physicists have raised. Nor will those who have watched the *Matrix* films, which imagine the universe as a giant piece of software where everything, including us, are just some lines of code.

## More and More Questions

Physicists have been struggling for decades with many questions and have found no answers yet. Why is time so different from space? In space, we can move about as we wish, but time seems to move only forward. What could be the reason?

**Is ours the only universe**? The very fact that our universe exists at all is a miracle. Just a slight change in the mass or charge of a particular type of particle or a tiny increase in the strength of one of nature's forces or just one more particle of antimatter, and there would be no stars, or planets or life. Did our universe win a lottery, where there can be only one winner? Or are there other universes too?

And finally, what caused the Big Bang that gave birth to our universe? Did the Big Bang create space and time itself, and then matter and energy? Does that mean there was 'nothing' before, a nothing our minds are incapable of grasping? Did our universe give birth to itself, or did something happen in the space-time continuum that caused it? And if that is true, what caused that cause?

The Nāsadīya Sūkta or the Hymn of Creation in the ancient Rig Veda asks:

But, after all, who knows, and who can say
From where it all came, and how Creation happened.
The gods themselves came later than Creation,
So who knows truly from where it has risen.

Where all Creation had its origin,
The creator, whether he fashioned it or whether he
did not,
The creator, who surveys it all from the highest heaven,
He knows – or maybe even he does not know.

But the story of humankind has always been about curiosity. Prehistoric humans wondered why a large glowing ball appeared and rose up in the sky every morning and then after some hours sank below the horizon. Today we are asking a far more fundamental, complex question: Is the universe real at all? Are we real?

We have come a long way.

We may still be nowhere close to finding all the answers, but we also know that we will never stop looking. Many of the greatest scientists ever born have said that the deeper they got into the workings of the universe, the more they were struck by the beauty of it and the more their wonder grew. They just kept finding more mysteries to solve, which only spurred them on to explore further.

We will never stop being curious. We know that we may never know the solutions to all the puzzles but there is joy in solving one and then finding another one that had been hiding under it and presents us with a new challenge. That is how we have always been as human beings and we should never change that trait. Solving those puzzles is the biggest 'thank you' we can say to the universe.

# A Note on the Authors

**Swagata Deb** has an MSc in Physics from IIT Kharagpur and a PhD from IIT Delhi. She was a senior scientific officer in IIT Delhi and has been a teacher for three decades. She is the author of several books for children, including *The Magical World of Mathematics*, which has been translated into Chinese, and *Goopy Gyne Bagha Byne and Other Stories*, which is now designated as a Puffin Classic. She is a painter and a Reiki healer.

**Sandipan Deb** is an IIT-IIM alumnus who quit corporate life to be a journalist and writer. He has been managing editor of *Outlook*, editor of the *Financial Express* and founding editor of *Outlook Money*, *Open* and *Swarajya* magazines. His books include *Fallen Angel: The Making and Unmaking of Rajat Gupta*; *The Last War*, a re-imagining of the Mahabharata in the Mumbai underworld; and *Suryavamshi: The Sun Kings of Rajasthan*, a translation of Abanindranatha Tagore's Bangla classic *Raj Kahini*.